The Legacy of
H. Richard Niebuhr

Harvard Theological Studies

Number 36

The Legacy of H. Richard Niebuhr

Edited by Ronald F. Thiemann

The Legacy of
H. Richard Niebuhr

Edited by Ronald F. Thiemann

Fortress Press   Minneapolis

In memoriam
Hans W. Frei
1922–1988

Library of Congress Cataloging-in-Publication Data

The Legacy of H. Richard Niebuhr / edited by Ronald F. Thiemann.
    p.   cm. -- (Harvard theological studies ; no. 36)
    Eight essays resulting from a conference honoring Niebuhr held in Cambridge, Mass. in September 1988.
    Includes bibliographical references and index.
    ISBN 0-8006-7084-1
    1. Niebuhr, H. Richard (Helmut Richard), 1894–1962--Congresses.
I. Niebuhr, H. Richard (Helmut Richard), 1894–1962. II. Thiemann, Ronald F. III. Series.
BX4827.N5L42 1991
230'.092--dc20   91–19505
                                         CIP

Contents

Preface

Too little attention has been given to the remarkable career of H. Richard Niebuhr (1894–1962). He was one of America's most distinguished theologians, yet more than a generation after his death, the full significance of his work remains to be measured.

In 1987, mindful of the twenty-fifth anniversary of his death, Harvard Divinity School and Yale Divinity School began planning a conference to examine the legacy of H. Richard Niebuhr and to asess his influence on modern theological scholarship. Over seventy scholars, students, colleagues and friends of H. Richard Niebuhr gathered in Cambridge for two days in September 1988 to pay tribute to his continuing importance, and to discuss fourteen essays and responses delivered by a group of scholars from various disciplines and fields.

The eight essays collected here retain the flavor of papers read at a conference. They examine issues raised in Niebuhr's own work, and develop his characteristic themes in new ways. H. Richard Niebuhr's scholarship was particularly distinctive because it extended over many fields which have become specialties in their own right. Niebuhr was not only a theologian; he was also a philosopher of religion, a historian of American Christianity, and a social ethicist. The papers gathered together in this volume reflect the range of his theological inquiry and the power of his insights. They also begin to review the extent of his ongoing contribution to theological thinking, and encourage further scholarship in areas related to his interests. In them the reader will find not only a reconsideration of Niebuhr's own theological statements, but also examples of the current diversity within theological scholarship and the many fields influenced by his writing. They make use of his words and thoughts as a starting point for studying the issues that were important to him and that continue to be important to the task of theology.

For H. Richard Niebuhr the primary task of theology was to understand the nature of human faith, and this conference also celebrated the publication of his only major unpublished manuscript, *Faith on Earth* (Yale University Press, 1989), edited by his son, Richard R. Niebuhr. Notions of trust, loyalty and community now so popular in contemporary theological discourse are analyzed in a remarkably prescient manner in this important volume.

This project, like so many others in theological education, simply would not have been possible without the support of the Lilly Endowment. In this instance the sponsorship was particularly fitting, since H. Richard Niebuhr more than anyone else inspired the Lilly Endowment to begin its work on theological education in 1958. I am especially grateful to Dr. Robert Wood Lynn, and also to all those who contributed either to organizing the conference or to bringing this volume into print: Constance Buchanan, Barbara Burg, Thomas Byrnes, Pamela Chance, Kimberly Cuddy, Missy Daniel, Mark Edwards, Cheryl Frost, James Gustafson, George Hunsinger, William Stacy Johnson, Leander Keck, Richard Niebuhr, Elizabeth Parsons, Stephen Peterson, Steve Prothero, Joe Snowden, William Spohn, and Michael West.

It remains only to note that H. Richard Niebuhr was the doctoral advisor for some of the most important church historians and theologians working in divinity school and departments of religious studies today, and many of them attended this conference. It was with the greatest sadness that we learned one day before the conference began that Yale theologian Hans Frei had suffered a stroke which proved to be fatal. Hans Frei's intellectual and personal ties to H. Richard Niebuhr were profound, and the reading of his paper on Niebuhr's legacy took on a special significance as a tribute to his own life and work.

H. Richard Niebuhr was a scholar of the greatest integrity and circumspection, a Christian intellectual who understood better than most "the never-ending pilgrim's progress of the reasoning Christian heart," in his own words, and the meaning of "faith seeking understanding," in the ancient words of St. Anselm. With the publication of this collection of papers we honor the richness of his legacy.

Ronald F. Thiemann
Dean
Harvard Divinity School

1

H. Richard Niebuhr
on History, Church and Nation

Hans W. Frei

A distant but very distinct fragment of a layer of memory remains from the days of World War II at Yale Divinity School. H. Richard Niebuhr, introduced by Ralph Gabriel, gave a lecture on post-war aims. (There were many lectures of this sort in those bleak days, when no decisive turn had come yet in the war's fortunes.) Apparently no manuscript or notes of his talk are extant, but the heart of what he said was powerful: Our innocence was gone, that innocence so much associated with our previous, semi-detached place among the great powers with whom we associated. We were now a worldwide empire. We could either exercise our position with restraint, or recklessly, with a heavy hand that could not rest until it had encircled the globe. That and that alone was now our difficult choice.

Like Britain in the tension between Gladstone's and Disraeli's foreign policy, we inched forward as nations usually do when their sense of insecurity increases proportionally to the growth of their power. We can recall a whole host of balkanized local area quarrels submerged and weirdly caught up in the threat of global Soviet

aggression. We can recall the bitter pill that Dean Acheson had to
swallow when he declared Korea outside the immediate interest-
sphere of the United States, and therefore was thought to have
encouraged North Korea to attack her neighbor to the south. The
very notion of the "containment" of Soviet expansion proposed by
George Kennan, chief of the State Department's defense planning
board, never very popular in government circles even in its heyday,
was abandoned under John Foster Dulles.

By a series of steps about which Reinhold Niebuhr would no
doubt have invoked the word "ironic"—he was himself, to some
extent, affiliated with Kennan's policy (Richard Fox, *Reinhold
Niebuhr* [New York: Pantheon Books, 1985], 238) —we were clearly
on our way to answering H. Richard Niebuhr's war-time query at
least in one respect: if self-restraint meant global self-limitation, it
was becoming more and more difficult. Increasingly the spirit, if
not the flesh, of American foreign policy was embodied in the
heady rhetoric of John F. Kennedy's inaugural address. Americans
were ready to go anywhere and pay any price to sacrifice for freedom, even if the burgeoning consumer culture—to say nothing of
the Vietnam war—questioned that flamboyant and heroic rhetoric.

In *The Rise and Fall of the Great Powers* (1987), the sales of which
testify to the timeliness of the debate which it and other works like
it have started, Paul M. Kennedy summarizes the situation of the
early 1970s with a quotation from Ronald Steel's *Pax Americana*
(1967):

> The U.S. had more than 100,000 soldiers in 30 countries, was a
> member of four regional defense alliances and an active participant
> in a fifth, had mutual defense treaties with 42 nations, was a member
> of 53 international organizations, and was furnishing military or
> economic aid to nearly 100 nations across the face of the globe
> (389–390).

Has our time come to fade gradually, though perhaps not as
dramatically and quickly as Great Britain earlier in this century,
from the global scene? Is our strategic situation perhaps as perilous
as our heavily dependent economic situation—a debtor to nations
overseas, especially to East Asian investors? Will our national role,
even apart from our defense budget capacities, be limited by the
power of new and rising demographic epicenters?

Let me be sure to state my argument carefully. I am not necessarily arguing that we were totally unrestrained in our policy as a new empire, only that we could not find any restraints less than those encircling the whole globe. In that sense, at least, Niebuhr's visionary plea received grim but clear answer.

From there I want to go on to state another tentative proposal, and tentative is all it ought to be. You will remember the early Reagan administration argument for drastically higher defense expenditures. The economic productivity of the Soviet Union was clearly shrinking, but that is precisely what made its empire so dangerous and so likely to be dangerously aggressive. *Mutatis mutandis,* if we are now decreasingly competitive, our industrial base inefficient in comparison with others, our indebtedness nearly out of control, and our military and non-military budgets dangerously imbalanced—though not as dangerously as those of the Soviet Union—why shouldn't the United States, precisely at this point and no matter how well-intentioned, be most dangerous to the balance of the world's precarious equation of power, even with recent improvements in Soviet-U.S. relations? Unless, that is, there is some privileged virtue to the species *homo americanus* (or *femina americana*), a speculative matter about which theologians may well have some built-in skepticism.

Given our open society, we do not have the luxury—as the Soviet Union, for instance, has—of foreign policy reversal without the danger of domestic face-saving embarrassment. The reversal of Soviet Afghanistan policy, difficult as it was, seems to have been child's play compared to the agony and bitter conflict of the U.S. reversal on Vietnam. The magic appeal to our "credibility" in foreign eyes, which Henry Kissinger invokes so ardently—credibility apparently as much for domestic appeal as for foreign policy reasons—might well make the Soviet Union at some crucial points a less adventuresome and dangerous nation than our own, a more open and electoral one.

I am not saying that these reflections are certain, dogmatic proposals. I am simply saying that, given H. Richard Niebuhr's farsighted remarks in 1943, he might well have taken the present time to be one in which the two terms, "responsible" and "restrained," were not only far more imperative but also far more difficult to achieve than we have witnessed in the development of U.S. foreign policy. In fact, the partnership between responsibility and restraint is so precarious as to be virtually unachievable without heavy countervailing foreign pressure on our own policy. A carefully modulated foreign policy for which a world of genuinely independent power structures exists, so that neither global policy integration nor a sense of our unlimited policy initiative will allow us to say that China or Iran are ours to "lose," is a hard thing to achieve for an empire which graduated to global power status only about fifty-five years ago.

To talk with confidence of the nation's duty was somewhat unusual for Niebuhr who, in striking contrast to his fellow clergymen, was quite restrained and circumspect in the agenda he set for the country as a whole. The nation was *the* crucial collective historical agent of the day. But at least Niebuhr had to share with his colleagues a certain kind of confidence in two respects, of which we are no longer sure.

First, the deadly serious and immensely learned search for a proper hermeneutic in our own day is a sign that on the foreign exchange markets, not only has the value of one kind of linguistic coinage gone up against others, but the mechanisms for exchange have become far more complicated. H. Richard Niebuhr and his contemporaries were more fortunate. The *lingua franca* between the mainline churches and responsible establishment leaders had not yet been broken (except for writers and readers of the *Partisan Review*). What we later came to call "civil religion" was an inheritance, still in place, of Puritan and evangelical traditions, in which the outlines and images of popular biblical history were still adequate to provide the mythology for the significant occurrences and turns of American history. This *lingua franca* was embraced by people like Walter Lippmann, who were pleading for a "public philosophy" in which people were public citizens rather than private believers, and as such were part of the linguistic compact. (In 1966, the acerbic, iconoclastic critic Edmund Wilson gave us in *Patriotic Gore* one long, grumbling and reluctant acknowledgment of this linguistic state of affairs.) It was a time when even rivals like Marxists were globally interpreted by American Christians not for their critique of ideology, but for their view of human nature, their practical vision of human agency, and the likelihood of achieving a just society under their scheme. The age of unbroken ideologies, each a means of support for interpreting the others in the same sweeping ways, was still in full hue and cry. The myth of the "American century" and of the "American way of life" was rife.

Second, the hermeuneutical plan onto which this biblical or biblically derived *lingua franca* was projected was human history, the future projections of which, to put the matter cautiously, were not totally veiled from human insight, so that the history of human affairs was not a mere trackless wilderness without any pattern whatsoever. We did not then look, as members of the *Annales* school do today, for the eventless or synchronic sequence of ordinary life in a stable society, in order to discover a meaningful basis for the pattern of difference and sameness in everyday life between then and now, to find out how it felt to be alive within a community of that time, compared to one here and now. They do so with the conviction that to look for anything more from history, such as a pattern of unique, unrepeatable events, is useless.

H. Richard Niebuhr shared the confidence in the diachronic, unbroken thrust from eventful past into eventful future, and the belief that this vision was part of the business of the interpreter of history. History, including American civil and religious history, as the course of human events, gave him the impetus for appropriating the patterns of language and interpretation which he chose in the late 1930s. It made available to him the partially but certainly not wholly revealed pattern in which the interpreter himself is directly involved in an intricate web that makes him both agent and analyst. Niebuhr wrote at the outset of *The Kingdom of God in America*:

> All attempts to interpret the past are indirect attempts to understand the present and its future. Men try to remember the road they have traveled in order that they may gain some knowledge of the direction in which it is leading, for their stories are begun without present knowledge of the end (1).

And again:

> The confused events of the past revealed a pattern to scribes and rabbis as well as to prophets and poets, and with that pattern in mind they made their choices in an ever critical present. In somewhat the same spirit we ask today whether there is in the history of American Christianity a pattern which may perform a similar function for us (2).

On that rare occasion during the war, to which I referred at the beginning, the Christian interpreter of history, the ethicist, and the theologian were all united in seeing the Christian as citizen in the public arena where all citizens meet, and where the citizen of a nation becomes a citizen, not merely of his own country, but of a global domain.

When H. Richard Niebuhr turned from *The Social Sources of Denominationalism* (1929) to the appropriation of a tradition in *Kingdom of God* (1937), he was deliberately moving from social to narrative or intellectual history. It was a move toward what we would call a "hermeneutical retrieval" or, in less grandiose terms, an affirmation that the language we use for our deepest religious convictions in our day is continuous with that of earlier ages, and that the earlier language is indispensible for us. Collective concepts available for these purposes—phrases such as "kingdom of God"—enter into a common time and linguistic frame of which we are all members, in other words, into a common "tradition." *Kingdom of God* is testimony to the compelling force of the bedrock, to the unavoidable and linguistically unsubstitutable language of tradition.

With that persuasion went another larger, and perhaps more dubious one: that the compelling force and connection of collective ideas runs through time for all those who inherit and loyally recreate and transform them. The history of ideas is not a self-engendered mystery with special, inherent explanatory powers (except in a limited way, explaining the relation between concepts). It is, rather, the retrospective understanding of a public tradition's moral and verbal coinage, and of our willingness to assume responsibility for it by entering into its usage. (This was in some ways a very un-Troeltschian affirmation, from a disciple of Troeltsch.) Niebuhr deliberately reversed the very route that most historians have traveled in recent years by moving from social to narrative or intellectual history. This reversal was also the adopted American son's ritual self-appropriation, so much more popular in America in that day than in ours, when the stories of our "foreign" traditions were incorporated into common, American ancestral lore. Today, in painful reversal, our stories are more apt to be those of alienation rather than appropriation of the common lore.

These grafts, however, were not entirely *de novo* for Niebuhr. Not only the content but also the method of this retelling took the form of the story. In method, it was at least in part an acknowledgment of the pilgrim or narrative shape embodied, perhaps more than in other sub-forms of Christianity, in the Calvinist tradition. Within English-speaking countries, it was also an acknowledgment of those characteristic Calvinist devices such as the allegory of *The Pilgrim's Progress*. The story told was that of God's active universal governance of all that he had made, and of his own unlimited, gracious, prevenient initiative toward all creatures.

In his interpretation of history Niebuhr was, despite his own denial, a man of powerful metaphysical vision. This vision, however, was not a shape to be separated out from the narrative shape in which we experience and retell the appropriation of any tradition. There is no identifiable metaphysical residue left over from the story of which it is a part. The two—the time-filled story, and its mysterious, overarching metaphysical or reality affirmation—are given together. Story images and general concepts are united but *never* convertible into each other. On the one hand there is a God, and furthermore, as Niebuhr once put it in a striking remark, "God is not simply up in heaven but in time itself" ("The Grace of Doing Nothing," in *The Christian Century*, 49 [1932], 380). In a series of late, tantalizing and undeveloped remarks, especially in *Radical Monotheism and Western Culture* (1960), Niebuhr indicated that the structure or principle of "being" and of the highest "being" are neither to be equated, nor are they to be disassociated—parallel to principles he had maintained in his value theory (*Radical Monotheism*, e.g., pp. 33, 38, 43, 46–47). This kind of repetitive, general (ontological) structure cannot in principle be anything more than a weak, retrospective, transcendental reading of the necessary ground for contingent, cumulative (ontic) relation of the responding creature with God. There is here, as in much of Niebuhr, a metaphysical vision for the fullness of divine initiative in relation to the created order, but its descriptive force is rendered solely by the given, specific "life story" of any creature or traditional group.

On the other hand we, the creatures responding to God, live wholly in time, and it is there that we encounter him: "What is past is not gone; it abides in us as our memory; what is future is not non-existent but present in us as our potentiality . . . Time in our history is not another dimension of the external space world in which we live, but a dimension of our life and of our community's being. We are not in this time, but it is in us" (*The Meaning of*

Revelation [1941], 69; see also all of chapter II, "The Story of Our Life"). Our time-filled, inescapably time-structured existence allows us neither to reduce the images of special occasions to general concepts nor to reduce concepts to images. Yet we cannot disassociate them; we can only tell the story of our communities as part of a fragmentary yet not wholly unknown, a hidden but genuinely universal narrative, a narrative the account of which is not only sequentially but synchronically unfinished.

Our story, our inquiry as observers into patterns which we as agents may act out, goes on, here in time, on the plane where God and humans meet. It is an inquiry into not only the church's but also our country's future, an inquiry into the polarity between the two, but always under the limited contingent conditions of response for our time to the creating, judging and redeeming work of God.

We know there are other contigent encounters than those of our story, so that each of them and the images through which we tell them cannot be reduced to those of other stories. Hence the unapologetic confessionalism of our understanding of the mediation of our understanding of God through Jesus Christ, our Christian "special occasion" of revelation. But hence, equally, the profound insistence that all attempts to universalize this story are unwarranted attempts to substitute our own religion for the full glory, the infinite, mysterious, unapproachable richness of the universal God who is active in and near to all things. It would be a characteristically Christian attempt to substitute our religious henotheism for the radical monotheism called for by loyalty to Jesus Christ.

By combining these motifs—the distinctive story of our specific confession within specific traditions, and its subordination to the sole glory and the universal, transcendent governance of the one God—Niebuhr entered the lists of the Reformed tradition, indeed the Reformed tradition as shaped, to his mind, in the early, perduring American Reformed tradition. He did this with a power and consistency that nobody in his generation in America could match, for his was an original refashioning and not a warmed over, traditional evangelical reaffirmation of that most mysterious word and experience of Christian confession. It was testimony to the experience of the sheer contingency of one's own life and of life among contingent creatures, and at the same time, it was effective witness to the sheer grace of God's glory. This was a refashioning message not addressed primarily to those evangelical conservatives who might receive it naturally—at least doctrinally, if not morally—but to those for whom this extraordinary claim and the very notions of a divine interruption of the human inititive and the throwing back of human questions as a divinely authorized force, were an absurd puzzle and an offense. In short, it was a message of unflinching, Reformed offense in the midst of a puzzled, liberal or post-liberal audience, including those Christian "existentialists" for whom "faith" is the highest existential act and creative force to which human beings must always be radically obedient. Hence Niebuhr's relative isolation among American theologians, but hence also the strength in his day, and yes, in our day, too, of the original shape of his theology.

In the quest to understand contingent existence as the manifestation of divine glory as sheer grace, Niebuhr was infinitely more than the ordinary, standard neo-orthodox, anti-liberal theologians, who in so many ways were really liberal theologians under the skin. "We have," he once said in a sardonic side comment on us all, "in our wisdom substituted for the holy God a kind, heavenly father" ("The Anachronism of Jonathan Edwards" [Address delivered at Jonathan Edwards' church on the occasion of the bicentennial of his death, Northampton, Ma., March 1958], p. 13). He was an original voice restating the Puritan heart of the matter for our day. In this service he found Jonathan Edwards, more than any other precursor, to be his mentor. Edwards had tirelessly expressed the same convictions in aesthetic, moral, biblical, historical and metaphysical coinage.

Niebuhr's only qualification of Edwards was that the sole mediation of that divine grace to us through Jesus Christ must be subordinated to the insistence that God alone is the universal source of all being and action. Niebuhr's view of Edwards was, perhaps, at least partially refracted through the later vision of Schleiermacher. But these two predecessors did, for all their differences, share a Reformed tradition. Refracted or not, it was Edwards, even if this subordination of Christology to theology did make for some genuine problems.

One must go on to ask whether even those problems weren't perhaps inherent in the American Puritan version of the Calvinist *soli Deo gloria*, or perhaps in Calvin himself. (Besides, to lean the other way and embrace the two, theology and Christology, as coequals, makes for other kinds of problems. That seems to be the nature of theology.)

In a passionate defense of Edwards, Niebuhr put the matter of the sheer grace of God's glory like this:

> What Edwards knew, what he believed in his heart and with his mind, was that man was made to stand in the presence of eternal, unending absolute glory, to participate in the celebration of cosmic deliverance from everything putrid, destructive, defiling, to rejoice in the service of the stupendous artist who flung universes of stars on his canvas, sculptured the forms of angelic powers, etched with loving care miniature worlds within worlds. In the light of that destiny, in view of that origin, because of the greatness of that calling, it depressed him, angered him that men should throw away their heritage and be content with the mediocrity of an existence without greater hope than the hope for comfort and for recognition by transient fellow-men. Man who had been made to be great in the service of greatness, had made himself small by refusing the loving service of the only Great One; and in his smallness he had become very wicked, covetous, of the pleasures that would soon be taken from him. *But in the end, man could not make himself small, Edwards knew, for the way of man is not in himself* (ibid., p.8–9).

To understand how this holy, mysterious power can be a universal, liberating source far, far beyond the scope of our selfish love to turn away from its narrow, parochial exclusiveness, Niebuhr reflected on the impact of this sheer grace on the inhibiting, selfish flow of our own contingent love:

> There is only one way out of the dilemma of human love. What if men could see that the universal, the eternal, the fountain and center of all being is their true good? What if they could learn to love their neighbors not insofar as these are persons, lives, minds, but because they are creatures of God and sacred by relation to the ultimate Being who is also man's true good? That is precisely the possibility that has been opened in Jesus Christ. In him the intention of the universe, to speak anthropomorphically, has become apparent; in his fate, even more than in his teaching, it has been made manifest that God is love. Through his life, death and resurrection, it has become possible to love the "Enemy" who seemed to destroy all his creatures but now is shown to be seeking their redemption (*Kingdom of God*, 115–16).

This eloquent passage shows the way in which the language and pattern of Niebuhr's thought reacted strongly to Jonathan Edwards, his own precursor, just as is meet and right in as strong a reader as Niebuhr was.

In the radical realism of this Reformed, Puritan *soli Deo gloria*, Niebuhr gave no quarter. It was, from beginning to end, the governing motif, the driving force of his theology. More than anything else this was the motif under which he read divine governance—and also divine judgment and crucifixion—in Scripture. It was also the prime universal principle under which he applied the images of biblical eschatology to an ever-present, merciful and objective, divine, universal, causal action. "Radical monotheism," as he came to call it,

> dethrones all absolutes short of the priniciple of Being itself. At the same time it reverses every relative existent. Its two great mottoes are: "I am the Lord thy God; Thou shalt have no other gods before me" and "whatever is, is good" (*Radical Monotheism*, 37).

It was an echo of Jonathan Edwards' "consent of being to being." To conceive of a more radically realistic theology than the yoking of these two affirmations would be difficult. In a way, one could say that Niebuhr risked almost everything not on methodological boldness, but rather on a somber, sober, even agonizing theodicy, as his great fondness for Spinoza's universalism, the wholly disinterested intellectual love of God, suggests. The images of creation, judgment and crucifixion, and redemption echo each other in a tightly linked continuum, where the hint of one divine action always carries, by dint of a mysterious, yet fit transcendent governance and initiative which we cannot fully grasp, the overtones of the other two.

Niebuhr thought hard upon the rift in our finite historical experience between the lack of power of the good, and the lack of goodness of temporal power. He saw in our natural experience the seeming two faces of God, as life-giver and as slayer. In this case, too, he refused to stay content within dualism and restrict God's action either to a thin, evanescently spiritual gruel within human spirituality, or else to turn it into a cruel, hard-nosed, objective, punitive, divine expedition on sinful humanity. It was a difficult row to hoe in between. Increasingly, especially in his reflection on the Second World War, the images of universal divine authority, of crucifixion, of divine-human sacrifice above all, and then, of the Calvinist understanding of penitence as the life-long act of the Christian person, moved together for him, into a mysterious pattern of coherence of Christian moral images in the moral life as told in the Christian story. (See Niebuhr's essays on the war in *The Christian Century*, May 13 and August 5, 1942, and April 28, 1943.) No set of events, including war, could conceivably echo a real absence of God from his world.

One needs to add that Niebuhr is quite unlike some present-day theologians for whom certain dogmatized categories or hypostatizations of creed and temporal history—"hope," "revolution," "resurrection," etc.—serve as an apologetic argument for the justification of divine goodness. Cognately, Niebuhr is equally unwilling to develop speculatively into a theodicy the parallel argument of divine fellow-suffering, whether through a process theory of divine possibility, or through some sort of equivalent inner-trinitarian speculation. In the face of all these temptations, Niebuhr remained unalterably agnostic. The price to pay for affirming the overwhelming, life-giving divine goodness is that of the sheer disinterested service of the only real God, and the condition of that service is one of total, life-long revolution in us—a repentance the initiator of which is not woman or man but God himself. Niebuhr would not go beyond these austere assertions, beyond the affirmation that through this quest for total revolution a mysterious sacrifice, in which a temporary design of fitness between God and man is woven together into one story of redemption, becomes manifest (at least for Christians). At that point he stopped exactly where his adopted Puritan ancestors and their ancestors would have stopped.

If Niebuhr was at once bold and agnostic regarding theodicy, he was far more cautious in adopting a methodology for articulating the principle of divine sovereignty, including that of theodicy. One sees a certain tension—yet it is rather more like a welcome disproportion—between his primary radically realist assertion of God's sovereign initiative, and the coordinate (or should one say subordinate) assertion of the religious or "faith" method under which to make this assertion. (The classic expressions of that ambivalence are contained in the magnificent supplementary essay, "Faith in Gods and in God," in *Radical Monotheism*; in "The Deity of

God," the concluding chapter in *The Meaning of Revelation*; and in *Faith on Earth*.)

Wherever Niebuhr has been treated either as a systematic theologian or put in the line-up of Protestant-liberal-neo-orthodox theologians, this theme has been developed, and I will not dwell on it. The common heritage of neo-orthodox and liberal theologians—from their Protestant origins, as they saw it, including their common rejections of classical theodicy as a valid problem—is that it is not God "in himself," but only "God revealed," or rather our relation with God, that is the object of our communion with God. "Faith" not only removes into a special, self-based kind of insight, but gradually, by a kind of merciless Kantian or perhaps Fichtean logic, is deconstructed into a totally originative human construction, in which the moment of divine revelation is no more than a self-positing move of the constructive intellectual capacity, in which the mind imagines or sets over against itself a transcendent "other" for its own regulating and constructing purposes.

A certain degree of caution is necessary before including Niebuhr in this line-up. Our reading of Niebuhr is onesided, if not wrong, for example, if we take the section in *Meaning of Revelation* on "History as Lived and as Seen," or on "internal" and "external" description, as methodologically nothing more than a Kantian dualism, an internal, traditional or self-participative perspective on the same historic scene which is described objectively under "external" causal categories. Actually, Niebuhr is usually restless with full, residual dualisms, moral as well as epistemological. Beyond that, in his interpretation of history, Niebuhr distinguished carefully between history as interpretation of the pattern or course of human events, and history as the story of the constructive reenactment of human understanding. The priority, especially if we take *Kingdom of God* seriously, belongs to the former, and the "internal" method certainly looks as if it were appropriate for this task.

Niebuhr's interpretation of history is a case of the disproportion or disequilibrium in which one has to choose between the priority of a radical realism on the one hand and a secondary, qualifying, critical, idealistic perspective on the other hand. This is not the case in his development of faith's self-understanding. As an interpreter of history, especially of our own traditions, Niebuhr asked himself—and us—to think more boldly, more realistically, than he did in the carefully, systematically balanced, critical-idealist analysis (or phenomenology) of faith, with its matching of phenomenal object to phenomenal reflection.

Of a piece with this disequilibrium in the interpretation of history, and probably more basic, is Niebuhr's developing anthropology in his final lectures on *The Responsible Self* (1963). It is almost startling to see the late, emerging consistency with perennial themes he had been pursuing ever since the 1930s. In his introduction to *The Responsible Self*, James Gustafson has rightly written that an imperative like, "Responsibility affirms—God is acting in all actions upon you. So respond to all actions upon you as to respond to his action" (*The Responsible Self*, 25, cf. 126), was "for most of H. Richard Niebuhr's students . . . the most memorable theme in his course of lectures on Christian ethics" (ibid.). One remembers from the course the sharp, almost colloquial question, preceding every moral response to God as Creator, Judge and Redeemer: "What is going on here?" The response was always carefully calibrated so that it was an answer not simply to a divine prevenient action, but to divine prevenience as refracted through our own interpretation of it. (For a suggestion of the intricacy of this relation, see the first two pages of Niebuhr's "Reflection on the Christian Theory of History," an undated paper among the H. Richard Niebuhr Papers, Yale Divinity School. See also *The Responsible Self*, 61–62.)

Niebuhr wanted to integrate the notion of the human being as a dual function-in-one, agent and interpreter. The two were one complex for him. Furthermore, in both aspects, separately and together, the person was basically a "dialogic" or "alternative" being, responding to a previous "alteraction." This anthropology takes (1) the image of man-the-maker with his freedom appearing "in this context as the necessity of self-determination by final causes" (*The Responsible Self*, 51) and (2) the image of man-the-citizen, living under law, asking for "what is possible to us in the situation in which we find ourselves . . . and not much more" (ibid., 52). In a very clear fit, it subordinates them both to the image of respondent to prior universal action on man—all in a way which these images would not fit if subordinated to a prior theology of radical and active divine prevenience. It is the doctrine of the human person—and of specific human communities—natural to a theology of radical monotheism. But it is a deliberate subordination, a kind of ruled priority in the explanatory use of Christian language, rather than a proposal for a systematic principle that would embrace both divine and human actions under one comprehensive heading.

There is no causal law and no law of theological perspective that would allow "response" to become part of a matched pattern of the interaction-in-one of divine and human agencies. (The center of the "disequilibrium" lies in the question whether "interpretation" is to be understood finally as a wholly autonomous response or whether, like agency, it is under the mysterious pattern of the divine Spirit as universal underlying prime cause. The issue is one completely natural to a theology whose greater impetus comes from the Augustinian, Reformation, and American Puritan traditions.)

One result of the priority of divine over human agencies, signalled by Niebuhr's choice of the "dialogic" or "responding" image over the other two, is the reaffirmation of some profound convictions that went back over the decades. The shock of recognition of what is to come is almost startling when one goes back to the early discussion between H. Richard Niebuhr and Reinhold Niebuhr in the pages of *The Christian Century* in 1932, and realizes how ill-matched they were. What must have been distressing to H. Richard Niebuhr was that, despite doubtless many years of discussion, his central concern, his most powerful persuasion of the prevenient initiatory action of God in time and in human events, was brushed aside by his brother simply as a casual *theologoumenon*.

Even then H. Richard Niebuhr said that God was a tangible, if mysteriously active structure and being, not a "third force" along-side of human beings and nature, but the "Other who is encountered in all human and natural challenges" ("Reinhold Niebuhr's Interpretation of History," 4, an unpublished paper delivered in 1949, also among the H. Richard Niebuhr Papers at Yale Divinity School). This is a reality on which all Christian assertions, both theological and moral, depend. Instead, Reinhold Neibuhr converted the dispute into that of an ethical imperative under a practical injunction—from a question of an ethics dependent on active, divine governance in history into an ethics under an absolute, fixed standard with one divine, efficacious aim in sight. His brother's claim, Reinhold Niebuhr said, was that "of dissociating a rigorous gospel ethic of disinterestedness and love from the sentimental dilutions of that ethic which are current in liberal Christianity" (*The Christian Century*, 49 [1932] 415). It is no exaggeration to say that

Reinhold Niebuhr took what, for H. Richard Niebuhr, was central
and motivating for Christian ethics, and turned it into a background belief whose sole utility was that of conceptually safeguard-
ing the imperative of "disinterested" and "sacrificial" love from the
sentimental simplification that liberal Christian moralists proposed
as substitutes for the ambiguities of rational public policy.

What was important here for H. Richard Niebuhr, first of all,
was that there was no sense of an aim in human history, understood as the course of human events. Furthermore, there was little
sense of history as "remembrance of things past." In an incisive
but profoundly generous critique of his brother's interpretation of
history, written about two decades after this *Christian Century* discussion, H. Richard Niebuhr said of Reinhold's view of history as
the process of later human reflection on past events: "Memory
interests him primarily as an aspect of man's freedom" ("Reinhold
Niebuhr's Interpretation of History," 2). What Reinhold Niebuhr
interpreted as history

> is not the "course of human events" nor yet the activity of the
> rememberer but the conception of social process as this is present in
> the mind of an ethical agent. Hence his questions about an interpre-
> tation of history are always questions about its ethical results insofar
> as it modifies conduct and somewhat, too, about its ethical origins,
> insofar as it has its sources in human faith or pride (ibid., 3).

This is Marx's or Comte's rather than Toynbee's or Collingwood's
way of coming at history. What is at stake here, not to put too fine
a point on it, is H. Richard Niebuhr's Augustinian view of human
freedom as always governed by some compelling motive force, and
Reinhold Niebuhr's modern view of human freedom, where even
the knowledge of ourselves as limited and not disinterested is simply a function of our own originating exercise of agential freedom.
"Man's freedom," said H. Richard Niebuhr of his brother's view,
"is not only the freedom of the knower, it is also the freedom of the
doer, though I am not quite sure how the transition is made from
the freedom man has as one who knows to the freedom which he
has as one who can change the course of natural events" (ibid., 5).

But for H. Richard Niebuhr we are not utterly originating, and in
that sense we are only categorically "free," both as knowers and as
rememberers or doers, and in the subtle unity of the two. This

strictly contingent independence holds true even in the self-criticism in which we supposedly adopt a divine, impartial, transcendent perspective upon ourselves. "Realized eschatology is realized theology," H. Richard Niebuhr said (*Responsible Self*, 167), making human, historic action contingent, qualified and limited, an initiative for the short or medium rather than long range, not only tactically but in principle.

On the other hand, Reinhold Niebuhr, *mutatis mutandis*, held the reverse coin of this persuasion. Whereas for H. Richard Niebuhr the theological assertion subordinated the ethical to an eschatological imperative, for Reinhold Niebuhr the opposite was the case. The ethical imperative totally subjected all eschatological perspectives to its own action frame. This is the very opposite of what H. Richard Niebuhr understood as "radical monotheism." An uninterrupted moral and self-starting initiative on the part of individual persons and especially of human collectivities was the explanatory framework for translating theological terms into the coinage of public moral action. We may not want to go quite as far as Reinhold Niebuhr's biographer, who summed up the 1930s discussion between the brothers as follows:

> In his undemonstrative, soft-spoken way . . . Helmut pointed out what Reinhold's other critics had not yet seen. Despite his fulminations against sentimental liberalism, against complacent faith in the redemptive character of human goodwill, Reinhold remained a thoroughgoing liberal. His God did not act in history. His faith was built not upon abandoning himself to God's will but upon the old liberal dream of transforming human society (Fox, *Reinhold Niebuhr*, 134).

But surely it is not exaggerated to say that, for H. Richard Niebuhr, theological and anthropological statements were more tensely and uneasily yoked. His effort at interpreting a Christian linguistic world so that it would be accessible to modern American audiences had to be more fragmented, qualified, partial and nuanced than his brother's. Both of these immigrant sons dedicated themselves to this interpretive task with a devotion and a searching quality that no other of their generation in America's mainline Protestantism could match. But for the one the liberal tradition, in rebellion as well as agreement, was the means of access to the modern, educated American mind, whereas for the other, even with all the phenomenological analyses of faith, it was finally more than anything else the highly risky and often rather lonely confidence that the Puritan-Protestant tradition provided the chief clue to the long-range continuity between Christian and American identities.

H. Richard Niebuhr's task, more than Reinhold's, was a lonely, difficult one. For when he looked around to see who was taking seriously the interpretation of his own *soli Deo gloria*—his persuasion of God's initiative not only in theological conception and judgment but in moral action—he immediately came upon Karl Barth, and what was then termed Barth's theological "actualism" or "occasionalism."

Niebuhr was deeply sympathetic even to Barth's radical assertion of the overarching efficacy of divine, predestinating grace. But increasingly what he could not swallow was the startlingly consistent Barthian identity of universal divine action with divine action in Christ alone. There were, for H. Richard Niebuhr, other mysterious forms of the *logos asarkos*, not only in the world's religions but in its philosophies, too. Between his brother's liberalism and Barth's consistent christocentric prevenience, Niebuhr's radically monotheistic affirmations had to wind their own unique way.

Barth once said, in characteristically biblical as well as Hegelian terms, that all we have to apply for theological interpretations are our own concepts, but that they themselves must die and rise again before they can be applied to their subject matter. Here Niebuhr said *no*. This was a miracle not at our disposal. As a result, his "faith method" stayed in place as a singular, religiously interpretive tool and a precondition for the knowledge of God, making him finally—despite all disagreements about the meaing of "radical obedience"—more sympathetic to Bultmann than to Barth. Niebuhr also insisted increasingly that Christian ethics are sufficiently part of a larger conceptual totality to allow comparison.

Barth, despite his denial that "Christology is anthropology," had understood all human beings in the light of this one man, Jesus Christ, as portrayed in the Gospels. The general concept of "man" had to die and rise through its appropriation and transformation in this unique christological image. Niebuhr, in his quest for both a universal form of theology and, in *The Responsible Self*, for a fitting, universal anthropology of the person as a responding creature, said no to this. The brief, brilliant, and tantalizing comment on "symbolic form" for Christians in the Earl Lectures was an answer to Barth. We are, in effect, dealing not with one symbol and image, as Barth proposed—though Niebuhr is like Barth in saying that we are dealing not with images that are simply allegories for general concepts—but with two that become interlocked. It is the interlocking synecdoches of Jesus Christ, first as a unique, non-generalizable instance of the image "responding person," and second as one who in his response is both prophet, priest and king, that together become the image of mediation between God and human beings in history. It is a set of images leading to an ethos that is not unique to Niebuhr, but bears resemblance, for example, to Jewish and Stoic ethics.

Niebuhr trod a delicate path between image- or story-shaped and universal ethics, and between universal and particular story-shaped theology. Unlike Barth, he refused to make a decision between a narrative and, shall we say, a trans-narrative, universal understanding of God's acts in history.

We can observe a parallel ambiguity in Niebuhr's subtle, rich and varied phenomenology of faith, with its universal characteristics fully affirmed and yet finally brought up short with the confession that the story of that faith's loyalty and trust to the loyal and trustworthy, transcendent source cannot be separated out from this particular history or narrative as it has been transmitted to us both through our tradition and our own personal placement within it. It is a dual line often repeated in his works. Indeed, in *Faith on Earth* the strong association of faith with christological images drawn from the biblical narrative may well be puzzling to non-Christian readers.

In this unique, profound path between Reinhold Niebuhr's type of undisrupted, liberal human initiative and Barth's consistently christocentric divine prevenience, I am left with an uneasy but hopeful sense. In the interpretation of history which is, even more than the analysis of faith, the very heart of Niebuhr's theology, the divine governance of the course of human events and our symbolic and interpretive reenactment of the past are not evenly yoked. Critical realism and critical idealism vie for priority. But, in contrast to *Meaning of Revelation*, *Kingdom of God* gives us a clue to priorities.

The narrative, interpretive retelling through such images as the kingdom of God provides a kind of bridge between these two parts of historical interpretation. Not that such images or even collective concepts have, as they do for the ordinary run of intellectual historians, a mysterious, explanatory power to substitute for social or causal explanation, but they are indispensible ways of understanding a tradition so that we can act within it for a common future. The kingdom of God was one of a number of mediating, interpretive principles drawn from tradition's usage that bridged the gap between the reality of divine agency in history, as course of human events, and the symbolic part played by our own faith's constructive act. The priority belonged to the radical realism of divine action, so that the critical-idealist method tended to become a qualifying safeguard of human limitation, the *nescio*, or "we don't know how our understanding fits our faith's claims," that has always, even before Kant, accompanied every Christian confession or universal divine causation.

In the choice of this priority and the consequent anthropology exemplified by the synecdoche of "responding person," the pressure is toward the denial that divine universal initiative and human interpretive construction are epistemologically equally matched. Neither as interpreter or metaphysical constructor of what has been in the past, nor as agent in present social process, am I totally free or purely originating. Once again, at least if we follow *Kingdom of God*, in both respects we are responding rather than initiating persons. Furthermore, the response is not simply temporally posterior to the reading of history as the divinely originated course of human events. It is located, instead, in a logically different plane to that of the divine initiation. God's objective action is a primary cause acting in, with, and through its secondary causal agencies. The classic disequilibrium of the Protestant tradition, expressed in its understanding of the Holy Spirit's activity, is always present in the background of Niebuhr's theory of history, no matter how carefully balanced the method of "faith" sounds. "Faith" is not finally a creative cause matched evenly against divine causation; it is, simply, a gift of God in repentance.

I want to conclude with a brief postscript on the Niebuhr lecture with which I began. It was a prescient lecture, given by a man deeply concerned with his nation's approaching role in history. But it was also the reflection of a man deeply persuaded that you and I do not finally govern the course of human events: God does. There is a powerful final sentence, of which Niebuhr would have approved, in a book he didn't much like, Austin Farrer's *Finite and*

Infinite (1943), written at the time of the German conquest of France: "... rational theology knows only that whether Paris stands or falls, whether men die or live, God is God, and so long as any spiritual creature survives, God is to be adored." Niebuhr, who rejected the distinction between rational and revealed theologies, would have added that not only "rational" but "revelational" theology, too, must make room for this confession.

The advice is tough, sober and stern; Reinhold Niebuhr would have thought it the poison of the theological paralysis of social action. One can understand why the anthropological theology of a Reinhold Niebuhr could be pulled in a liberal and neo-conservative direction. On the one hand, there was the appeal to restraint contained in emphases on ambiguity and self-criticism; on the other hand, there was not only the inevitability or realism of collective self-interest, but above all the rejection of denying the uninterrupted freedom of initiatory human action.

It is a different story with H. Richard Niebuhr's short-range historical action, in principle limited by divine governance, in which our "alteractions" are limited in, with, and through agencies other than our own, and they by ours. It is a different matter also when the chief created agencies under God's governance are not simply the political collectivities of nations and empires, but when divine action is located in the uneasy, at first sign almost ludicrously illbalanced "polarity" (as James Gustafson has rightly said, a favorite word of Niebuhr) between the nation, or other assorted social collectivities, and the church. "Radical monotheism" insisted on this polarity because the universality of one sort of group is always henotheistic (we might as well say idolatrous, including, of course, the church). "The task of the present generation," Niebuhr could say at about the same time he was working on *Kingdom of God*, "appears to lie in the liberation of the church from its bondage to a corrupt civilization" (*The Church Against the World* [1935], 124). But twenty years later, under different circumstances, he could speak equally well (with recent, rather distasteful ecumenical discussions in mind) of Christ-centered and church-centered "henotheism," and say that "history is reinterpreted so that the story of the mighty deeds of God in creation, judgment, and redemption is replaced by church history or 'holy history'" (*Radical Monotheism*, 58–59). It is virtually impossible to think of H. Richard Niebuhr's theology and ethics leading to neo-conservatism.

Why be a poet, Hölderlin asked, in these non-lyrical times? Why, we might ask of H. Richard Niebuhr, be a theologian in our utterly untheological times? I think he would have made short shrift of that question. He would have asserted, I believe, that our responsibility to affirm the glory of the Lord, and his glory alone, has not been altered one whit, and that this remains our duty in propitious or unpropitious times. In the name of the Puritan heritage itself, he would have rejected the notion of a special covenant between God and the American nation. A sobering call to take our place in an increasingly pluralistic world with a humanitarianism modified by Chrisian hope, and to restrain the global anxieties unleashed by global power would, I think, have appealed to him.

We have a more modest mission to play without losing the distinct role the Christian tradition has contributed to the best of American ideals. We are not a specially chosen nation, but we might, under appropriate circumstances, be an internationally useful people. If the Puritan ideal of America as a city set upon a hill now recedes, Niebuhr would have been confident that other aspects of the same tradition could have handled the now less ardent dreams. I am sure he would have rejected the kind of special-election-in-disguise claim that Puritans resorted to in their times, the so-called "jeremiad," which has so fascinated commentators from Perry Miller to Sacvan Bercovitch.

We theologians could have expected from Niebuhr an unsentimental call to do our duty, no matter whether we were finally of weighty cultural influence or not. To remain in our particular station in America, as testifiers to that almost lost Puritan heritage of the universal governance of God in the Reformed tradition, which can only be articulated in the polarity of the church and nation, with responsibility to the interaction of the two, even if it becomes culturally and linguistically more difficult than it was in the past—that is our heritage.

To be sure, with his carefully modulated pluralism, Niebuhr would have said that other people have other stories, and even Chrisians in other lands may have other responsibilities to their civilizations and, through them, to their God. Some may have more conservative responsibilities, for instance, in Poland; others may have to urge the "preferential option for the poor" in a systematic way. But for us in the right now increasingly residual "mainstream" American Protestant heritage, the imperatives of our

Puritan ancestors still hold us to the dual responsibilty to church and nation under mysterious, divine prevenience, even if that language is restricted right now to an increasingly smaller circle.

In the service of this heritage, Niebuhr might have asked us at least to consider the possibility that the more modest scope of a renewed Puritanism might have a natural parallel—the possibiity of a new, far more limited role for the American nation. He might well have suggested that this modest scope might actually be more liberating than the careening, constantly burgeoning anxiety of power, and that this possibility might be a positive alternative for a public theological posture between those two notorious collective mood swings—national self-hatred and national self-glorification—those twin evils which afflict American Christian moralists so much in our day. There is a great deal of unadvertised, unglorified reconciliation to be done "in church and civil state."

Niebuhr might well have approved Karl Barth's insistence that there is no natural line of affinity from liberal politics to the witness of the church. (One remembers Niebuhr's wartime remark that many liberals have never forgiven God for making a nationalist U-boat captain, Martin Niemöller, witness to him.) But he might equally well have agreed with Barth that with caution, care, forethought and luck, there might just be an affinity the other way around: that a gospel of the universal, present, governing glory of God might have more to do with a carefully circumscribed progressive politics than with either a theology of revolution or some other political theology, which some fellow-Christians have proposed to us (thus far with little effect, it must be admitted, or else with the battlements of neo-conservatism). One step at a time, no more than that for the task of public theology; but always with the protest against national self-aggrandizement and idolatry in mind. It is a slim line, but a goodly cause.

In H. Richard Niebuhr we had a teacher who represented, more than anyone else in the mainline Protestant church tradition and its educational institutions in this country, a fiercely radical monotheism which was at the same time an equally positive affirmation of God's active lordship in our midst. Niebuhr believed it to be a faithful tradition for Christians on these shores to hold. None was greater than he in upholding this simple, yet complex theological mission. It is a distinctive vocation that must not be lost.

2

Response to Hans Frei

Gordon D. Kaufman

Hans Frei has presented us with a masterly essay on H. Richard
Niebuhr. In particular, his insistence that the real foundation of
Niebuhr's entire theological program is to be found in his rock-firm
faith in the One God, creator and redeemer of all that is, seems to
me right on target. Frei is also basically right, I think, in holding
that Niebuhr's powerful sense of the meaning of faith expressed
itself in a kind of epistemological realism with respect to God. He is
certainly correct in seeing a strong tension or polarity between this
realism and the critical idealism found in much of Niebuhr's writing: in his reflections on human faith, for example; in his so-called
"faith-method" in theology; in his contrast of "internal history"
with "external history"; and in his forthright acceptance of a version of historical relativism.

I want to devote a good portion of my remarks here to this tension and its significance. But before I turn to that, let me thank Hans
Frei for such a moving evocation of Niebuhr's spirit and ideas, an
evocation that cannot but lead any of us who were his students to
meditate deeply on the respects in which our own theological
efforts fall short of the example set by our revered teacher. Hans

Frei's essay gives us all much food for reflection and thought, and for this we must be deeply grateful to him.

There is not sufficient time here to summarize the main points Frei made in interpreting Niebuhr. With most of them I find myself largely in agreement, and I have no desire to quibble over details of interpretation. But I do want to raise some questions with respect to a certain onesided emphasis in Frei's overall argument about the realism/idealism polarity in Niebuhr's thought.

Doubtless he is correct to hold that for Niebuhr himself the reality of God—and the consequent priority of God over everything creaturely—was absolutely central. For this reason there could be no question about whether God was to be understood, for example, as a reality essentially "posited" by faith, as many liberals and, indeed, many neo-orthodox theologians held, as Frei points out, with faith thus being given a kind of priority over God. On the contrary, as Frei wrote, "In the radical realism of this Reformed, Puritan *soli Deo gloria*, Niebuhr gave no quarter. It was, from beginning to end, the governing motif, the driving force of his theology."

Frei believes, therefore, that in Niebuhr's own faith and thinking there was a significant disproportion "between his primary radically realist assertion of God's sovereign initiative, and the coordinate (or should one say subordinate) assertion of the religious or 'faith' method under which to make this assertion," and that "the priority belonged to the radical realism of divine action, so that the critical-idealist method tended to become a qualifying safeguard of human limitation." Frei is probably correct to contend that Niebuhr understood himself to be holding to some such disequilibrium between the realistic and the idealistic moments in his thought. There seems to be much evidence of this, and the framing of his ethics in terms of the idea of response was intended to underline just this point. We have been taught in recent years, however, that searching for authorial intention is not by itself an entirely adequate hermeneutical procedure. There is always a good deal more going on in a text than the author realizes, and some of this may even be contrary to his or her conscious intentions. If we look at the realism/idealism polarity in Niebuhr's thought with this point in mind, we may have to reach a different conclusion regarding this matter of priority—or at least we may find ourselves seeing this issue in a somewhat different light than is urged in Frei's paper.

Frei does not give as full an analysis of Niebuhr's "faith-method" and its implications as he does of Niebuhr's conviction about God's absolute priority over everything human. The most I can do is remind us of the great circumspection with which Niebuhr approached the metaphysical affirmations of faith, whenever he discussed them. There was no question in his mind that faith makes ontological or metaphysical claims about God's reality, God's oneness, God's gracious governance of all creation, and so on. But it was equally clear to Niebuhr that all these affirmations were matters of *faith*, not knowledge. They were matters learned through a historically relative "inner history" (as he put it in *The Meaning of Revelation*), not matters publically ascertainable or confirmable. They were claims clearly disputable from other points of view, which must themselves be given respectful attention and consideration—claims which, thus, we can only "confess" to be what we see from our faith standpoint.

This faith confessionalism which Niebuhr articulated involves a certain agnosticism (as Frei also notes), and it drives on toward an inescapable relativism, as Niebuhr himself often acknowledged. I want to suggest now that this agnosticism and relativism undercut any and all absolutistic faith claims. Frei indirectly recognizes this. He reminds us, for example, of how distasteful Niebuhr found the "Christ-centered and church-centered 'henotheism'" of much of the ecumenical theology of his time. He points out that Niebuhr rejected Karl Barth's confidence that God miraculously makes our theological concepts adequate to their divine subject matter, as "a miracle not at our disposal," and he reports Niebuhr's "profound insistence that all attempts to universalize this [Christian] story are unwarranted attempts to substitute our own religion for the full glory, the infinite, mysterious, unapproachable richness of the universal God."

The relativism (and implicit agnosticism) of Niebuhr's confessionalism and his doctrine of "inner history" were not, of course, nihilistic. Niebuhr saw clearly that we can and we must live out of the traditions of meaning and value with which our inner history equips us; they are, in fact, the main sources of orientation and order for our lives. But the relativism involved in his conceptions required Niebuhr (and requires us) to tread very cautiously in making claims about the ultimate, the universal, the really real.

If we take seriously Niebuhr's interpretation of Christian faith in terms of the notion of internal history—with its not fully public, but nonetheless powerfully illuminating events providing fundamental orientation for life—it is difficult to see on what grounds it could be claimed that faith provides privileged and certain insight into the ultimate mystery behind all being and value. Niebuhr did not want to get into a defensive posture of that sort with respect to Christian faith. That is why he described his stance as resolutely "confessional." But precisely this confessionalism, it would seem, precludes just that confident epistemological realism which Frei found to be central in Niebuhr's theology.

Do not misunderstand me. I am not disagreeing here with Hans Frei's point about Niebuhr's own personal convictions regarding the reality of God—although one cannot help but wonder a bit about this also, in view of the centrality which the problem of theodicy had for Niebuhr, as Frei rightly points out, and in consideration of the powerful existential questions and doubts which must have been connected with his reflection on that issue. Whatever may be the case about Niebuhr's own inner struggles with the problem of evil, however, there is no question that Frei is correct to hold that as a theologian he affirmed, often in very powerful language, the reality of the Calvinist/Puritan God. The words which Niebuhr wrote in tribute to Jonathan Edwards surely apply equally well to himself: "What Edwards knew, what he believed in his heart and with his mind, was that man was made to stand in the presence of eternal, unending absolute glory, to participate in the celebration of cosmic deliverance from everything putrid, destructive, defiling, to rejoice in the service of the stupendous artist who flung universes of stars on his canvas, sculptured the forms of angelic powers, etched with loving care miniature worlds within worlds."

My question is not whether this really was the very heart of Niebuhr's personal faith, but rather, does the critical-idealist side of Niebuhr's thought permit one to make straightforwardly realistic claims about these deepest mysteries of life and death? Does it really justify—as Hans Frei, and perhaps also H. Richard Niebuhr, wished—giving prominence (as Frei has done) to those impulses in faith which desire an epistemological realism with respect to what it calls "God"? Or must we be much more circumspect than this—

once we have learned from Niebuhr's relativism and confessionalism and agnosticism—in the ways we use, and the claims we make
for the great symbols and stories of the Christian tradition?

In raising these questions I do not mean to suggest that we
should adopt what Frei calls the "merciless Kantian or perhaps
Fichtean" position, according to which "the moment of divine revelation is no more than a self-positing move of the constructive intellectual capacity, in which the mind imagines or sets over against
itself a transcendent 'other' for its own regulating and constructing
purposes." If we must retreat from the epistemological realism of
Frei's interpretation, it does not follow that we must move to the
opposite extreme which takes faith to be somehow simply and
straightforwardly creative of its object.

As Niebuhr (and Frei) rightly hold, human beings are essentially
responsive realities, not sheer creators of their own lives and worlds;
and faith, also, must be understood as essentially *response*, not pure
spontaneity. But what is it response to? Rather than answering
immediately, "*God*, as understood in the Christian tradition," it
would be more accurate, I think—and more Christianly modest—to
interpret faith at its most primordial level as response to the ultimate mystery of life, response to our sense of an ultimate *unknow-
ing*. For as Niebuhr wrote in his essay on "Faith in Gods and in
God" (*Radical Monotheism*, 122), "We may not be able to give a
name to [this final reality], calling it only the 'void' out of which
everything comes and to which everything returns, though that is
also a name."

Human faiths everywhere, in their response to the primordial
mystery of life, have created pictures of the world and stories of the
human place within the world. These pictures and stories gave
shape and meaning to the ultimate mystery—shape and meaning to
which faith could then further respond, thus producing forms of
life with widely varying flavors, practices, and institutions, as many
diverse religious traditions gradually developed and spun their distinctive ways through history. But no matter what the metaphors,
images and concepts used to domesticate the ultimate mystery,
they have never proved capable of fully comprehending the heights
and depths of experience, or of anticipating the interruptions, the
surprises and calamities of history.

Our humanly created schemes of meaning never succeed in

doing justice to the ultimate mystery of things. So our various faiths are repeatedly forced to respond again and again, attempting to fine-tune their images and symbols, or perhaps proposing new metaphors or concepts which will bring radical transformation to the web of meaning. But through all of this, the distant horizon of our living, our knowing, our believing, remains the profound void of which Niebuhr spoke. Among these pictures and stories and symbols, created in and through faith's response to the mystery which surrounds and continually breaks in upon us were, of course, those which came to constitute the Christian tradition, and which have thus been used to articulate the self-understandings of Christian faith.

Faith must certainly always be understood as *response*; it is not self-initiating. Therefore any interpretation of Christian faith that does not acknowledge a decisive priority (over our own initiatives and actions) of action upon us from beyond is misleading and false. But it is an oversimple parochialism, too easily dismissive of the multiplicity of ways of being human as we are aware of these today, that quickly identifies, in the conventional terms of any religious (or secular) tradition, that reality to which faith is responding. If we are to face up to today's problems of religious and cultural pluralism, we must seek to frame our understandings of both human beings and the world in less imperialistic, more open ways. Niebuhr's sense of human historicity, relativity, and a certain proper agnosticism can be an important guide for us in this venture—but not if it is subordinated to an overly realistic reading of traditional Christian metaphors and symbols.

Hans Frei quite rightly sets his interpretation of Niebuhr's theology within the context of the world-historical situation of his time; for Niebuhr believed that Christian faith and theology provided a standpoint for interpreting "what is going on" in the world. Frei also points out early in his paper that the climate of the times has changed radically from Niebuhr's day. The Christian story no longer provides the *lingua franca* in terms of which our culture at large understands itself and its world, and the meaning of human life and human history now seems in many respects more obscure and perplexing than it did even two generations ago.

But from these important changes Frei does not seem to draw any conclusions whatsoever about the way in which Christian faith should be interpreted today. Indeed, he holds that we theologians "in our particular station in America" should remain essentially "testifiers to . . . the universal governance" of the Puritan God. This is certainly an astonishing conclusion, in view of the degree to which traditional theological symbolism has become suspect today—inside the Christian churches as well as outside. Not only does that symbolism seem archaic, or unintelligible, or unfashionable, but we can now see how dangerously oppressive and destructive it has often been in the past. One thinks of its paternalism, its sexism, its authoritarianism, its Christian triumphalism and tendencies toward imperialism, its easy subversion by racists and nationalists, its anti-ecological anthropocentrism and anthropomorphism.

Hans Frei has suggested that, in contrast to what has happened to Reinhold Niebuhr's thought in recent years, "it is virtually impossible to think of H. Richard Niebuhr's theology and ethics leading to neo-conservativism." But is that really true? Or does the litany of evils which I have just recited not suggest that a continued uncritical theological employment of traditional Augustinian/Calvinistic/Puritan images and symbolism may in fact authorize and reinforce neo-conservative tendencies with respect to some of the most difficult and perverse problems facing humankind today? This may be precisely the historical moment when theologians are called to recognize more forthrightly than H. Richard Niebuhr did (or than much of the Christian tradition has done), that it is no longer fitting to seek to see our world, and our human place within the world, largely in terms of the *political* symbolism traditionally employed by Christian faith—in terms, that is, of notions like the "kingdom of God" or the "divine governance." Rather, we must now learn to understand and express Christian faith in ecological, evolutionary and social metaphors and images more consonant with modern understandings of our human situatedness in the world.

Is it really good enough for us Christian theologians, as we take part now in what is increasingly becoming a pluralistic conversation world-wide, to attend only to *our* traditional way of seeing things, to confine ourselves to what is revealed only in *our* inner history? Or is it incumbent, particularly upon us theologians of the Christian churches, to listen carefully to what others say about what has been revealed in their inner histories, opening ourselves increasingly to the symbolic resources of other traditions, as we all seek to move, in our now irreversibly global village, toward a life together before and within the ultimate mystery of things?

H. Richard Niebuhr's theology can offer us much guidance in addressing these sorts of issues, but it can do so only if we are willing to accept for ourselves what he called "a permanent revolution of the mind and of the heart, a continuous life which opens out infinitely into ever new possibilities" (*Radical Monotheism*, 126).

3

Theology as Responsible Valuation or Reflective Equilibrium: The Legacy of H. Richard Niebuhr

Francis Schüssler Fiorenza

In the controversies between the moderns and ancients during the Renaissance, it was said that when one stands on the shoulders of giants one can see farther than they. H. Richard Niebuhr is such a giant. We struggle to climb on his shoulders. Yet we discover that he saw farther than we do. He saw clearly what we are just beginning to see. As we begin to talk about the critique of foundationalism, about narrative and story, and about social analysis within historical studies, we discover paths that Niebuhr already marked out.

As a constructive theologian, Niebuhr was more than our immediate predecessor. He was our vanguard. Today, in systematic and fundamental theology, we face issues at the foundation of Christian theology. What is the nature of theology? What is its task and method? Which criteria does it employ? We seek to answer anew these questions, for challenges have emerged to traditional as well as modern answers. Current philosophy challenges whether knowledge has secure foundations. It points to the problems of relativism, the dilemmas of historicism, the role of interpretive communities, and the relation between theory and practice. All these issues form the challenge called the "critique of foundationalism."

Niebuhr pioneered in struggling with the issues implied in the critique of foundationalism. Such a term was not in use at his time. Yet many of the issues were without doubt present. Niebuhr struggled with them and made constructive proposals. His proposals strike at the center of contemporary theological debates. They are indeed still relevant today. Therefore my paper will analyze Niebuhr's theology in relation to the issues that the critique of foundationalism raises. It will show that Niebuhr's understanding of the nature and criteria of theology was sensitive to the issues that this critique raises.

The Foundations of Theology and the Critique of Foundationalism

Contemporary epistemology has developed a basic critique of foundationalism that has challenged and influenced much of theology.[1] This critique stems from our awareness of the historicity of the subjective and objective world. Appeals to data, facts, and historical events do not refer to mere data or brute facts. They refer instead to interpreted data. Appeals to human subjectivity do not refer to an *a priori* consciousness. They refer instead to a historically conditioned consciousness. Interpretations take place within a larger framework of knowledge and beliefs. As a result, the critique of foundationalism raises questions not just about the foundations of knowledge and belief, but also about relativism and truth, interpretive communities and truth, and the relation between theory and praxis.

Theology and the Foundations of Knowledge and Belief

The critique of foundationalism has emerged only recently as an explicit and programmatic theme in theology.[2] Nevertheless,

---

[1] The classic expression of the critique of foundationalism is Wilfrid Sellars's critique of the myth of the given. See Sellars, *Science, Perception and Reality* (London: Routledge & Kegan Paul, 1963), especially the essay "Empiricism and the Philosophy of the Mind."

[2] See Francis Schüssler Fiorenza, *Foundational Theology* (New York: Crossroad,

Niebuhr's understanding of the foundations of Christian theology anticipated it in several ways. He did not see reason, revelation, and scripture as foundations removed from the limits of history and society that could thereby provide absolutely independent and objective foundations for Christian theology.[3] His analysis of Kant, Descartes, and empirical theology underscored central elements of the critique of foundationalism. He accepted the Kantian insight into the need for transcendental categories to interpret reality. Yet he did not accept these categories as universal. He insisted instead on their relativity. Likewise he criticized Descartes' use of methodic doubt to secure a certain foundation for attempting in vain to remove human subjectivity from the limits of history.

Niebuhr criticized the transcendentalism of liberal theology. Yet he did not simply repeat the standard neo-orthodox objections against anthropocentricism in theology. He underscored instead the historicity of categories of thought. In addition, he criticized the foundationalism of empirical theology. Contrary to its empirical claim, such a theology fails to grasp that persons perceive nature within the framework of interpretive and historical categories. An empirical theology cannot, therefore, provide the secure and valid foundations that its seeks through its allegedly empirical scientific method.

Relativism and Historicity

Niebuhr also faced the challenge that relativism poses for the theological task. He did not search for some Archimedian point outside the web of history. Instead he acknowledged the historicity of Christian theology. He recognized the finitude of all human knowl-

---

1984) and Ronald Thiemann, *Revelation and Theology* (Notre Dame: University of Notre Dame Press, 1985).

[3] Donald E. Fadner, *The Responsible God: A Study of The Christian Philosophy of H. Richard Niebuhr* (Missoula, Montana: Scholars Press, 1975), 51. Fadner argues that Niebuhr thinks that the Christian philosopher renders intelligible "our common human experience." C. David Grant, *God the Center of Value: Value Theory in the Theology of H. Richard Niebuhr* (Forth Worth: Texas Christian University Press, 1984) criticizes Fadner for overlooking "the fine distinction between common experience and common structures of experience" (21). My interpretation likewise argues that Niebuhr's acknowledgment of the historical and social conditioning of all experience enables him to distinguish between an appeal to common structures of human experience and common human experience.

edge. He insisted on the relational nature of religious knowledge. He used the term "confessional" in his early work to express this relational nature of faith and theology. Theology is historically and socially conditioned, as all human knowledge is. Theology, moreover, reflects the relational nature of religious valuations. Therefore, theology should criticize any absolutization of finite social, cultural, national values, including theological notions and religious values.

Thirty years ago, Paul Ramsey criticized Niebuhr for his concern with relativism. He objected that relativism is religiously unnecessary, theologically unwarranted, ethically dangerous, and historically false.[4] Despite such objections, Ramsey correctly observed that Niebuhr's central concept is more a "relational objectivism" than a "relativism." Today, however, we seek a position "Beyond Objectivism and Relativism."[5] We need to learn from Niebuhr's resolution in facing the problem of relativism.

Interpretation and Community

Confronted with the historical and social conditioning of ideas and values, philosophers have not simply become aware that human knowledge lacks secure and certain foundations. They have sought to go beyond relativism and objectivism by analyzing discursive practices and interpretive communities. American philosophers as diverse as Michael Walzer and Richard J. Bernstein (the latter appealing to Jürgen Habermas and Hans-Otto Appel) have pointed to the interpretive role of communities. They claim that this interpretive role provides a key that can unlock the problems of pluralism and relativism. Such an understanding of the interpretive role of communities is already present in Niebuhr's writing. Likewise, contemporary theologians such as Johann Baptist Metz and Helmut Peukert have emphasized the universality of the human community. They have called for a solidarity with suffering victims and with the dead. Such an appeal for solidarity with those who suffer and with the dead was central to Niebuhr's understanding of the universal community.[6]

---

[4] Paul Ramsey, "The Transformation of Ethics," in Paul Ramsey, ed., *Faith and Ethics: The Theology of H. Richard Niebuhr* (New York: Harper & Row, 1957), 140–72.

[5] The title of Richard J. Bernstein's important survey of the contemporary reflections on relativism, *Beyond Objectivism and Relativism: Science, Hermeneutics, and Praxis* (Philadelphia: University of Pennyslvania Press, 1983).

[6] H. Richard Niebuhr, *The Responsible Self: An Essay in Christian Moral Philosophy* (New York: Harper and Row, 1963), 94–107.

Niebuhr's view of community was sensitive to the issues of relativism and foundationalism. On the one hand, he affirmed a radical monotheistic faith over against any social henotheism. He criticized all absolutizations of institutional Christianity that made the particular denomination the end of Christianity. On the other hand, Niebuhr distinguished between internal and external history. In so doing he profiled the importance of internal history. He emphasized the role of narratives, and insisted on the indispensability of participatory knowledge for the the Christian community's self-interpretation.

Niebuhr emphasized both the relativity of all institutional religious communities and the centrality of a community's internal history. A community exists with a historical standpoint and with particular beliefs. Yet such a community, Niebuhr argued, should bring its beliefs into dialogue with other communities, with diverse communities, both religious and secular, and with the universal community of humankind.

Theory and Practice

The relationship between theory and practice is becoming increasingly central to diverse philosophical and theological positions.[7] Today many complain of the fragmentation of theology. They lament the splintering of Christian theology into diverse disciplines, especially the division between systematic theology and ethics or moral theology. Several contemporary movements seek to remedy the situation. Hermeneutical theory stresses the significance of application for understanding. It shows the significance of Aristotle's practical philosophy for interpretation. Latin American liberation theology incorporates the Marxist understanding of the practice-theory relation in its critique of ideology. And a renewed interest in the American pragmatic tradition seeks to integrate its notions of practice and community for the formation of theory and values.

Here, too, Niebuhr appears as our vanguard. He argued that theory and practice were constitutively intertwined. He advocated the interrelation between theology and ethics. He appropriated the

---

[7] Francis Schüssler Fiorenza, "Theory and Practice: Theological Education as a Reconstructive, Hermeneutical, and Practical Task," *Theological Education: Supplement* 23 (1987) 113–41.

moral theory of value, current in his time, for Christian theology, moral philosophy, and Christian ethics. In his Cole Lectures at Vanderbilt in 1960, Niebuhr described his earlier work: "It appeared also in the tendency to deal with theology in the perspective of ethics so that the basis of much theology was value judgment theory or the theory of conscience."[8]

Niebuhr's understanding of faith and ethical responsibility combined theological and ethical reflection. His theory of valuation joined theory and practice. His ethics of responsibility united theoretical and practical reason. His understanding of the criteria and nature of theology rested precisely on his appropriation of a theory of valuation, conscience, and responsibility from practical and moral philosophy.

Universality and Particularity in Christian Theology

Dean Thiemann's invitation suggested that my paper should examine Niebuhr's understanding of "Loyalty to the Truth: The Universal and the Particular in Christian Theology." The tension between the universal and the particular comes especially to the fore in the critique of foundationalism, for this critique challenges whether secure subjective or objective foundations for universal truth claims exist. Therefore the critique of foundationalism serves as a background for an analysis of Niebuhr's conception and practice of theology in relation to the universality and particularity of truth claims.

Such an analysis leads to a comparison between his understanding of theology as a responsible valuation with its reflective method, and the method of broad reflective equilibrium, as employed in recent ethical, philosophical, and theological writings.[9] Such a comparison raises this basic issue: how does loyalty to truth within a theological adaptation of a theory of value compare with

----

[8] Cole Lecture I, p.18, on microfilm in Andover Library of the Harvard Divinity School. Niebuhr described value judgment theory as a corrective to pragmatism's excessive emphasis on action.

[9] This method has emerged in discussions of John Rawls, *Theory of Justice* (Cambrige: Harvard University Press, 1971). For a bibliography on the discussion on broad reflective equilibrium, see the final section of Francis Schüssler Fiorenza, *Foundational Theology*.

loyalty to truth within a theological adaptation of a method of reflective equilibrium? How do these different approaches resolve the tension between particularity and universality? How do these different approaches take into account the contemporary critique of foudationalism?

My interpretation of Niebuhr's theology focuses on these questions conceptually rather than historically. Therefore it does not examine the shift from his earlier to his later writings. His adoption of a phenomenological method in his later writings, indeed, had important consequences. His own self-description of his development, however, was basically correct, and there does exist a fundamental continuity.[10] Nor does my interpretation explore Niebuhr's background. There had been a tendency to stress the Continental background (i.e., Troeltsch) and to read Niebuhr in relation to crisis theology (i.e., Barth). Today one underscores the influence of American theology and philosophy (i.e., Jonathan Edwards, Josiah Royce, and George H. Mead). Nor does my interpretation compare him to other historical figures, as I have already compared his interpretation of America with Shailer Mathews's interpretation.[11] Instead, my interpretation analyzes his systematic and conceptual position. It especially examines the relation between the universal and particular as its appears in his understanding and practice of the nature and criteria of theology.

Niebuhr's Conception of Theology

How did H. Richard Niebuhr define Christian theology? What is distinctive about Christian theology, its purpose and content, its context and criteria? Niebuhr wrote, "Theology is differentiated from other kinds of intellectual activity by being the reflection that goes on in the Church; it is therefore the kind of thinking that is directed toward God and man-before-God as its objects and which

---

[10] It is important that Niebuhr recognized later that Barth's description of nineteenth-century theology, especially Schleiermacher and Ritschl, was one-sided. See his essay "Reformation: Continuing Imperative," in the series, "How My Mind Has Changed," *The Christian Century* 77 (1960) 248–51.

[11] See Francis Schüssler Fiorenza, "American Culture and Modernism: Shailer Mathews' Interpretation of American Christianity," in Thomas E. McFadden, ed., *America in Theological Perspective* (New York: Seabury Press, 1976), 163–83.

is guided by the love of God and neighbor."[12] This sentence compacts several elements of Niebuhr's conception of theology.

Theology as Theocentric and Catholic

Theology is a kind of thinking, a reflective and intellectual activity that has as its object and direction God and persons-before-God. Theology is thereby differentiated from other activities in two respects. First, it is differentiated in regard to its object. Theology differs from all other disciplines that may have objects other than God or humans-before-God. The love of God might motivate these disciplines, yet their reflection and study of these objects abstracts them from the ultimate object. Instead their reflection focuses on some aspect of them "without making them objects of devotion."[13] Theology's intellectual activity fosters the intellectual love of God and persons-before-God.

Second, theology is differentiated as a discipline. Theology, as an intellectual discipline, is a pure science. Niebuhr's characterization of theology as a "pure science" and as a "disinterested science" is related to his conception of theology's object. Theology is for the sake of God and for persons-before-God, and not for the sake of any lesser interest. The words "pure science" and "disinterested science" may be misleading. The attributes "pure" and "disinterested" could easily be misunderstood as meaning "unrelated" or "uninterested." Niebuhr intended to affirm that theology is theocentric: its interest is theocentric. Disinterestedness means that theology puts aside all secondary, extraneous, and private interests. It focuses on God and persons-before-God for the sake of its ultimate object of love, God.

The relation between the human self and God is at the center of Niebuhr's affirmation. He used the term "disinterested" for two basic reasons. The first reason stems in part from his conviction that the objectivity of science is grounded in disinterestedness. Hence if theology is to be objective, it should be disinterested. To the extent theology shares the scientific ideal of other disciplines, it is disinterested.

Yet there is a second reason. Niebuhr followed Karl Barth in

[12] H. Richard Niebuhr, *The Purpose of the Church and Its Ministry* (New York: Harper & Brothers, 1956), 109.
[13] Ibid., 110.

equating "interested" with a "lack of objectivity."[14] As Barth did, Niebuhr often equated "interest" with human self-interest that is egoistic and relative.[15] Theology as disinterested expressed the universality of theology.[16] It did not imply "disinterestedness," or the study of God in isolation from humanity. Instead, Niebuhr constantly affirmed that the proper study of theology is God and persons-before-God.

As an intellectual discipline, theology is reflective and employs a reflective method. Theology shares in all the activities of the intellect. It compares, abstracts, analyzes, and relates in order to seek unity and coherence. Theology seeks this unity insofar as it elaborates the coherence of the manifoldness of human experience in relation to the ultimate God. As an intellectual activity, theology has a universality of scope and a universality of coherence as its goal.

Yet theology is also a love, in that theology is a participatory knowledge. Love has a noetic character. To describe theology as an intellectual love is to describe not only the motive and goal, but also the character of theology. Niebuhr argued that if a love other than the love to the Ultimate Being guides theology's intellectual activity, then theology as an intellectual activity "cannot see or understand what love understands."[17] In other words, unless theology is guided by what I have called above "theocentric interestedness," it fails to see what it should see and understand.

Theology is, therefore, a participatory knowledge. It not only reflects upon faith, but it is a reasoning that takes place in faith, a reflecting that takes place within a loyalty and commitment. Niebuhr's understanding of theology as a committed and participatory knowledge enabled him to explain the role of theology not

---

[14] For an analysis of the relation between objectivity and interest, see Francis Schüssler Fiorenza, "The Responses of Barth and Ritschl to Feuerbach," *Sciences religieuses/Studies in Religion* 7 (1978) 149–66.

[15] "Jonathan Edwards," in Waldo Beach and H. Richard Niebuhr, eds., *Christian Ethics: Sources of the Living Tradition* (New York: John Wiley & Sons, 1955), 380–89.

[16] In Niebuhr's moral theory of conscience, the notion of "disinterested" is also central, and serves a role similar to Mead's notion of "impartial observer." See especially Niebuhr's manuscript, "Conscience: Its Role in Ethics and Religion" in the microfilm collection in Harvard Divinity School's Andover Library.

[17] Niebuhr, *The Purpose*, 109. See also *The Meaning of Revelation* (New York: Macmillan, 1941), 67–100.

only in relation to the purpose of a theological school, not only in relation to the purpose of a church, but also in relation to other human activities and endowments. In his own words, "Though intellectual love of God and neighbor is not the supreme exercise of love, yet it is required and possible since man is also mind and does not wholly love his loves if his mind does not move toward them. He cannot truly love with heart, soul and strength unless mind accompanies and penetrates these other activities as they in turn accompany and penetrate it."[18] Such an understanding of theology undergirds the purpose of a theological school, which was for Niebuhr "that place or occasion where the Church exercises its intellectual love of God."[19]

Theology's distinctive commitment and loyalty comes to the fore in its activity and the goal of its activity. Since theology seeks to interpret the intelligible coherence of everything in God, it has a loyalty that is both universal and ultimate. This universal ultimacy of theology distinguishes its commitment not only from forms or reflection that are less than universal, but also from misdirected forms of theology. A theological reflection loyal primarily to some particular value fails its distinctive end. Theology, therefore, has a criticial function. It exercises this critical function toward such misdirection, toward the practices and activities of the church. It must take care that worship, proclamation, pastoral care, counseling, and community organization do not degenerate into particular practices that become as ends in themselves rather than in relation to God.

In summary, the primary purpose of theology flows from the love of God and neighbor. Its reflection on the coherence of all things in God corresponds to the monotheistic faith in God. Its primary purpose of reflective loyalty to the universal ultimate requires the critical examination of all cultural values and ecclesial practices in relation to its universal and ultimate loyalty, to God.

The Communal Context of Theology

Christian theology, as Niebuhr insisted, is that "reflection that goes on in the church." He affirmed that "it is necessary to think of the theological enterprise in terms of community and as an affair of

---

[18] Ibid., 111.
[19] Ibid., 110.

genuine back-and-forth communication."[20] Niebuhr's understanding of the nature and scope of the community corresponded to his conception of the back-and-forth communication of theology. His conception of community was nuanced. It recognized the particularity of communities, yet it also acknowledged the universality of the human community and the overlapping of particular communities. Although Niebuhr located Christian theology within the Christian community, he underscored the relation between the Christian community and the universality of the human community so as to eschew sectarian conceptions of Christian theology or the Christian community.

People live within various historical and social communities. These communities are like overlapping and interacting circles in dialogue. There is the community of those believing in God. There are Christian communities, from biblical times to the present—without excluding post-biblical communities. There are modern Christian communities interacting with other communities in the world. Niebuhr's emphasis on theology's "back and forth communication" becomes especially important in his analysis of the relation between the modern Christian community and two of these communities—the biblical community and the wider community of the contemporary world.

The biblical communities have a special significance for Christian theology. Nevertheless, the interaction between modern and biblical communities is not a one-way movement. It is not simply that the Bible speaks to the theological student. The theological student also speaks to the Bible.[21] The interaction is such that new meanings are constantly emerging.

The Christian community stands also in communication with the larger communities of the world. There is a long tradition of interaction between the Christian community and communities of secular learning and other religious traditions. Christian theology shares the responsibility of interpreting the Christian faith to the larger community of the human world. It is also responsible for interpreting the large community of the world to the Christian community.

This responsibility to the universal human community before

---

20 Ibid., 119.
21 Ibid., 120.

God is the other side of Christian theology's responsibility to understand all reality in relation to the One God. The Christian faith is a particular faith, but its loyalty is to God as the ultimate unity behind the manifold of all reality. Its theology has a responsibility not only to the particular but also to the universal community.

Theology as the Practical Reasoning of Faith

A third element of Niebuhr's understanding of Christian theology is the notion of theology as the practical reasoning of faith. The reason of theology differs from that of science. Niebuhr stated, "It is the same reason and yet reason has varieties of work, and theology is a little more like ethical reasoning than it is like scientific reasoning. The reasoning of practical reason is where you are concerned with value."[22] The presuppositions of Niebuhr's understanding of theology as the practical reasoning of faith lie in his conceptions of the theory-practice relation and of the relation between theoretical and practical reason. These conceptions provide the background theories to his notion of theology as a reflective method and as the practical reasoning in faith.

Niebuhr developed a dialectical relationship between theory and practice. He sought to avoid either an intellectualist or a pragmatic approach. The intellectualist affirms that one first conceives the idea (e.g., the idea of God, salvation, or church). Only after one has understood the idea is one then moved to love and obedience, faith and edification. The pragmatic viewpoint considers theory irrelevant or secondary to practice. It looks upon practice as a beginning and end in itself. In contrast to both views, Niebuhr affirmed that theory and practice are constitutively intertwined. There is never a moment of action without reflection. Nor does reflection take place independent of action. Instead, reflection is a necessary ingredient of action. It serves action by abstracting, relating, comparing, criticizing, and discerning patterns. The action of a disciplining will and a guiding love in turn are also inherent in reflection. Both reflection and action are interrelated.[23]

Likewise, Niebuhr distinguished but did not separate theoretical and practical reason. Theoretical reasoning focuses on the observa-

---

[22] See the panel discussion with Pope, Boell, Calhoun, Fairbank, and Pollard, "Science and Religion," *Yale Divinity News* (January 1960) 3–21; quotation is from p.19.

[23] Niebuhr, *The Purpose*, 125–34.

tion of facts rather than on values. It accompanies the observation of the behavior of other beings. Practical reasoning entails values. It accompanies our own decisions and commitments. Yet as fact and value cannot be separated, neither can practical and theoretical reasoning be divorced from one another. In politics, ethics, and religion, practical reasoning does not exist without theorizing, just as in science, theoretical reasoning does not exist without making choices about values.[24]

These distinctions should be correctly understood—as distinctions, but not as separations. A separation would not only overlook their intertwinement, but would also destroy the unity of the self. The distinction between speculative and practical reason and between theory and practice, like the distinction between body and mind, is often misunderstood as separation. Niebuhr conceded that previously he had understood the distinction between the theoretical and the practical with reference to the subjective activity of reason. Reason as theoretical is speculative, contemplative, or observing. Reason as practical is the subjective activity of reason engaged in doing. Instead of distinguishing the theoretical and practical in terms of subjective activity, Niebuhr later suggested that one distinguish them "by reference to their objects as *facts* and *values*."[25]

The distinction between the theoretical and the practical enters into Niebuhr's understanding of the task of diverse intellectual disciplines. Science is a theoretical discipline, and yet it manifests a "trust-loyalty." A similar "trust-loyalty" is present in religion, recognized in politics, and exhibits the struggle of the various forms of faith. Therefore, "science which makes universal truth its cause takes its place alongside universal religious faith and the politics that is guided by universal loyalty."[26] The difference between practical and theoretical reasoning lies in their relation to universality. Science as a theoretical science has universal intent, for it seeks the universal in the particular. It examines the particular for patterns that others can verify. It seeks to relate patterns so that each particular occasion is interpreted with reference to the more general, and

[24] H. Richard Niebuhr, *Radical Monotheism and Western Culture* (New York: Harper & Row, 1970), 78–79.

[25] Niebuhr, *The Responsible Self*, 83.

[26] Niebuhr, *Radical Monotheism*, 88.

even beyond the general to the universal.[27] Practical reasoning, in contrast, analyzes the part. It interprets the whole from the perspective of that analysis. In sum, scientific theoretical reason interprets the particular by looking for the universal in the particular. Theology as a practical reasoning uses the particular to interpret the universal.

This understanding of the theory-practice relation highlights Niebuhr's conception of theology as practical reasoning in faith. The method of theology as a reflective method does not argue from God's existence to God existence as Barth does. Instead it underscores the "personal practical trust" in God. This trust does not so much affirm the existence of God as it affirms God's relation to us. Our knowledge of God is not an abstract knowledge. It is a limited knowledge in faithful trust and loyalty.[28] Faith is not, as in Thomistic faculty psychology, an act of the will or heart that supports the intellectual assent of the mind. Instead faith is that relation of trust within which knowledge of God arises. Therefore for Niebuhr no knowledge of God exists apart from a relationship of faith.

Thus a specific and particular relationship provides the basis for theological reflection. Out of the practical and concrete relationship of Christian faith, Christian theology seeks to interpret the whole or the universal as practical reasoning. Christian theology moves from its concrete faith and practical reasoning to the whole, rather than from the whole or the universal to the particular.

Niebuhr's Criteria of Theology

The nature of theology, its end and purpose, its context and community, and its particular faith and commitment serve to establish the criteria of theology. Secondary literature on H. Richard Niebuhr sometimes objects that he does not provide sufficient criteria for concrete individual decisions.[29] Such charges, however, should not lead one to overlook that Niebuhr implicitly and explic-

---

[27] Niebuhr, *The Responsible Self*, 88.

[28] For an examination of Niebuhr's method as well as of continental influences see Hans Frei, "The Theology of H. Richard Niebuhr," and "Niebuhr's Theological Background," in *Faith and Ethics*, 9–116.

[29] Thomas R. McFaul, "Dilemmas in H. Richard Niebuhr's Ethics," *The Journal of Religion* 54 (1974) 35–50.

+ Cady in this volume

itly used several important criteria for the constructive theological task: theocentrism, comprehensiveness or catholicity of vision, integrity of self, and fittingness.

Theocentrism

Niebuhr's first criterion, theocentrism, was the central and pervading criterion of his theology. It means that the foundation of any responsive evaluation is God. God is the absolute source of all valuation. Thus God is that by which all else has value. This primary criterion eschews criteria outside of and independent of the valuation of God. It insists that Christian theology must take seriously its task of fostering the intellectual love of God and neighbor, and must criticize any form of theology or church practice that substitutes a proximate goal for the ultimate goal.

In contrast to polytheism and henotheism, theocentrism thereby affirms the universality of radical monotheism. Henotheism is particularistic insofar as it takes some finite particular and relative value, and makes it absolute. Henotheism claims that the values of particular political, social, ethnic, and gender communities are absolute. Theological reflection must, therefore, point out that such social, cultural, national, and even religious values are finite. It identifies them as such. This criterion of theological reflection alerts one to polytheism and henotheism. It especially flags henotheism because the tendency to elevate social faiths to values and principles predominates.

Comprehensiveness or catholicity of vision, the second criterion,[30] is the other side of theocentrism. This criterion is also the other side of radical monotheism, and protests the particularism of polytheism and henotheism. Catholicity consists in loyalty to the universal. It refuses to elevate the particular and finite to the universal and absolute. Niebuhr's appropriation of the criterion of comprehensiveness and universality was carefully nuanced. He distinguished Christian moral philosophy from Christian theology. Philosophy as well as Christian moral philosophy develops a form of analysis that applies "to any form of human life including the Christian. All life has the character of responsiveness."[31] Neverthe-

---

[30] For Niebuhr's understanding of the term "catholic vision," see "The Gift of the Catholic Vision," *Theology Today* 4 (1948) 507–21.

[31] Niebuhr, *The Responsible Self*, 45–46.

less, even such a moral philosophy acts "as though that life were nonhistorical, as though the ideas . . . referred to the pure emotions of nonhistorical beings or to pure concepts."[32]

Theology, however, unlike metaphysics and ontology, does not abstract its discourse about God from "discourse about the objective reality, God."[33] Niebuhr's understanding of theological method as "reflective method" or "faith method" does not take as its starting-point a universal or comprehensive viewpoint. It does not seek, as other sciences might, an external meta-theory or comprehensive framework that can establish the validity of individual theory. In his owns words, "reflection on faith, like every other reflective inquiry, must begin . . . right in the middle of things. It cannot 'begin at the beginning' of the dialogue between subject and object or of the dialogue between self and other selves."[34]

Niebuhr's method in theology, as distinguished from his method in moral philosophy, did not begin with common human experience as an unhistorical phenomenon. His phenomenological analysis affirmed the historicity and relativity of all human experience at the same time that it sought to show that trust and loyalty are present in a variety of human endeavors and experiences. Christian theology employs a reflective method that contemplates a concrete historical faith. Nevertheless, it does not eschew the universal, as a sectarian and particularistic version of theology might. When Niebuhr as a Christian theologian reflected on Christianity's historical and particular religious symbols, he started out from the concrete particular. He related that particular to other particulars and to the universal.

In short, Christian theological reflection relates its concrete historical symbols to what is universal. It seeks to show that the religious symbol can serve as the interpretation of that universal.[35] It is this catholicity of vision that serves to criticize the idolatries of denominationalism, institutionalism, and confessionalism,

---

[32] Ibid., 46. Niebuhr also describes *The Responsible Self* as an essay in the "prolegomena to Christian ethics," because it abstracts from the life of the Church (86).

[33] Niebuhr, *Radical Monotheism*, 12.

[34] H. Richard Niebuhr, *Faith on Earth: An Inquiry into the Structure of Human Faith* (ed. Richard R. Niebuhr; New Haven: Yale University Press, 1989), 24–25.

[35] See the appendix, "Selected Passages from the Earl Lectures on The Responsible Self," in Niebuhr, *The Responsible Self*, 149–78.

as well as those of biblicism and excessive Christocentricism in Christianity.

Fruitfulness for Integrity of the Self

Niebuhr's argument for the superiority of the symbol of responsibility over the symbols of maker and citizen displays his use of the criterion of fruitfulness or fertility. The symbols of human being as maker and citizen, representing, respectively, the teleological and deontological theories, are helpful in understanding and orienting ourselves. However, Niebuhr argued, "they remain images and hypotheses, not truthful copies of reality . . . something of the real lies beyond the borders of the image; something more and something different needs to be thought and done in our quest for the truth about ourselves and in our quest for true existence."[36] Niebuhr affirmed, as ever, the reality beyond the images and symbols that one uses. The truth of these symbols and images lies not simply in their correspondence to reality, as if images and symbols were copies of reality. Instead the truth of these symbols consists in their fertility for self-definition and for self-orientation within reality. The truth of these symbols consists, thereby, in their adequacy to self-interpretation and to praxis.

The symbol of responsibility highlights aspects of self-definition and of self-defining conduct that are obscured when the images of the self as agent or doer are translated with teleological or deontological images.[37] In addition, the symbol of responsibility assists human persons in achieving that unity of self called personality. This unification of the manifold into a personal unity is a task of moral as well as psychological theory. The symbol of responsibility is, therefore, more "fruitful" for this task than are the other symbols.[38] In the face of suffering, the self experiences that which is beyond its control. The self experiences that which frustrates its movement for the self-realization of its total potential. Again, the symbol of responsibility is more adequate to the task of self-definition than other symbols.

Likewise, in analyzing the theory-practice relation, the determination of the center of value, the relationship between the good,

---

[36] Niebuhr, *The Responsible Self*, 56.
[37] Ibid., 57.
[38] Ibid., 54.

right, and value, and the importance of a monotheistic faith, Niebuhr underscored this criterion. The integration of personality and the unity of the self in its self-definition serve as a central criterion that displays the adequacy of his theological affirmations. Adequate theological reflection and a fitting response enables the self to integrate its diverse role into an integrated unity. Niebuhr's analysis of the triad of faith (its relation to self, community, and cause) commends itself as the more comprehensive and adequate interpretation of the self in trust and loyalty to others and to the most inclusive environment. The correlation between the self and the One beyond all finite particularities is the response that enables the person to act as an I, as a unified rather than a fragmented and splintered self.

Fittingness and Responsible Valuation

The notions of "fittingness" and "responsible valuation" are perhaps less criteria than they are the result and sum of Niebuhr's previous criteria. Niebuhr understood the human self as agent caught in the web of historical, social, and natural dependencies. His theories of agency as responsive, and of responsible valuation reflect this understanding. This responsiveness is translated in Niebuhr's theology as a responsible relation. His moral theory characterized a proper response as a "fitting response." His reflections on Christian theology characterized it as a "responsible valuation."

In moral theory, the term "fitting" has several resonances. It recalls the Stoic notion of a "cathekontic ethics."[39] It also gives the impression that Niebuhr's ethical stance was "intuitive" in the sense that W. D. Ross defines right in terms of the "suitable."[40] Such an impression, however, is a misreading of Niebuhr. A "fitting response" involves several elements: alteraction, attentive interpretation, accountability, and social solidarity. In contrast to alternative ethical positions, it shifts the emphasis. A fitting response does not begin with a set of established universal moral principles in order to then apply these principles to a concrete particular case. Instead, it begins with a description and interpretation of the

[39] Richard E. Crouter, "H. Richard Niebuhr and Stoicism," *Journal of Religious Ethics* 2 (1974) 129–46.

[40] W. D. Ross, *Foundations of Ethics* (Oxford: The Clarendon Press, 1939), 146.

concrete situation or event. A fitting response asks the questions, what is going on, what is God's action in this situation, and what is God's intention in this event? The answer to what constitutes a fitting response is determined in part by one's interpretation of the situation or event, and thus is not simply intuitive. It must take into account the other three criteria (theocentrism, comprehensiveness, fruitfulness to the self).

For Niebuhr the problem of moral norms was "on its objective side the moral problem of the one in the many . . . the problem of discerning one action, one intention, one final context of all the actions upon me, whether these issue from natural powers or from men, from It's or Thou's."[41] He was acutely aware of the complexity of discerning what is fitting. Ethical responsibility consists not just in seeking the good as superior to the right, as in teleological ethical systems. Nor does it consist simply in affirming the right as superior to the good, as in deontological systems. Instead, ethical responsibility consists in recognizing that which "fits into a total interaction as response and as anticipation of further response, is alone conducive to the good and alone is right."[42]

Within Christian theology, the major category is responsible valuation. Since Christian theology, as the practical reasoning in faith reflects on faith's valuation, its reflective method raises the issue of responsible valuation and seeks to balance objectivity and subjectivity. On the one hand, it reflects on the presence of faith on earth. On the other hand, the triadic structure of Christian faith (to self, others, a cause) is no merely subjective experience. It is a response to the Transcendent. It is an acknowledgment of the Absolute. A responsible valuation places all human valuations of self, others, and a cause in proper relation to this real transcendent Absolute, God.[43]

Method of Reflective Equilibrium and Niebuhr's Method

These criteria indicate the complexity of Niebuhr's approach to theological criteria. This complexity is often overlooked by persons

---

[41] Niebuhr, *The Responsible Self*, 125.
[42] Ibid., 61.
[43] See "The Structure of Faith," in *Faith on Earth*.

who latch on to the term "confessional theology" and neglect everything else Niebuhr wrote. But the complexity suggests to me that something approaching a method of reflective equilibrium was operative in the way Niebuhr did theology. The complexity of Niebuhr's actual practice of theology is obvious in his appropriation of value theory.

Value theory was an important theological and philosophical current. It provided a background to Niebuhr's thought, yet he did not accept it uncritically. He criticized it sharply while appropriating the categories of value and valuation for his own constructive theology and moral philosophy. An explicit comparison of the method of reflective equilibrium with Niebuhr's understanding and practice of theology will illustrate similarities and differences, advantages and disadvantages.

The Method of Reflective Equilibrium

Reflective equilibrium is a current method in epistemology, legal, political, and moral theory. John Rawls's use of this method in *Theory of Justice* has led to considerable discussion and debate. Like any method, reflective equilibrium is open to diverse interpretations, criticisms, modifications, and applications. It provides a tool for analyzing ethical and theological approaches, especially Niebuhr's approach to theology. In addition, since the method of reflective equilibrium deals with the critique of foundationalism, it offers an alternative to Niebuhr's reflective method and responsible valuation in regard to the issues that this critique raises.

Broad versus Narrow Reflective Equilibrium

The basic idea of reflective equilibrium arises within the pragmatic tradition of American philosophy, yet it moves decisively beyond pragmatism. Its roots go back to John Dewey's conception of reflective experience. Decisive developments take place in Nelson Goodman's riddle of induction and in Israel Scheffler's analysis of the relation between commitments and justification within the anatomy of inquiry. Also influential for its development are Morton White's arguments for the significance of the so-called "Duhem-thesis" for justification in ethical theory. This thesis argues that scientific explanation and predication put to the test a whole body of beliefs, rather than just the one belief under test.[44]

The basic idea of reflective equilibrium is that justification consists in a continual mutual adjustment or a mutual correction of principles and considered judgments. This method acknowledges the historicity of both our principles and considered judgments in that it takes seriously the problem raised by Nelson Goodman's "new riddle of induction." Goodman argues that the problem of justifying an induction is not above and beyond the problem of defining or describing valid induction. Indeed, the problem of defining confirmation displaces that of confirming justification. Confirmation is not simply a descriptive task. Instead, confirmation is necessarily constructive and projective.[45] Seeking to avoid the weaknesses of conventionalism and utilitarianism, Goodman maintains that appeals to consequences raise again the issue of justification and the principles of selectivity.[46]

Israel Scheffler and John Rawls suggest that in moral theory a constant interplay takes place between initial commitments and justifications within the total context of one's beliefs and within the search for a coherence of one's knowledge, beliefs, and practices. One constantly seeks to bring one's considered judgments into reflective equilibrium with one's account of individual situations and with one's principles, until a coherence between principles and considered judgments emerges.

Rawls's initial appropriation of reflective equilibrium met with success and crticism. The criticisms focused on his notion of the original position, with its veil of ignorance as the fulcrum point, and on the absence of background theories about human nature and personhood. These criticisms led to the proposal in the ensuing discussions of what is called a "wide or broad reflective equilibrium" in contrast to a "narrow reflective equilibrium." The notion of broad reflective equilibrium emphasizes that moral knowledge is based not solely on considered judgments and principles, nor simply on mutual adjustment between principles and practices of

---

[44] Morton White, *Toward Reunion in Philosophy* (Cambridge: Harvard University Press, 1956), 251–91.

[45] Nelson Goodman, *Fact, Fiction, and Forecast* (Cambridge: Harvard University Press,1983), 59–83.

[46] See Israel Scheffler's commentary on Goodman from *Anatomy of Inquiry*, now in *Inquiries* (Indianapolis: Hackett, 1986), 165–74, especially in regard to Goodman's understanding of projectability.

experience. Moral knowledge entails certain background assumptions and theories that impact upon the mutual adjustments and considered judgments. These background assumptions also affect the reflective equilibrium. For example, assumptions about the nature of the human person enter into the equation in discourse about justice.

Broad reflective equilibrium is both a consequence and a consistent development of narrow reflective equilibrium. It takes into account much more the historicity of knowledge and the holistic features of changes in beliefs and values. It brings more clearly to the fore the Kantian dimensions of Rawls's own appropriation. It underlines the need for a historically and hermeneutically oriented understanding of the method of reflective equilibrium. Several contemporary authors have consequently extended the method. Norman Daniels has sought to develop a broader conception of reflective equilibrium.[47] Ronald Dworkin applies a method of reflective equilibrium to the interpretation of law. Such interpretation seeks the integrity of law in reinterpreting and reapplying law.[48]

Theology as Reflective Integrity or Reflective Equilibrium

My formulation of foundational theology has sought to employ the method of reflective equilibrium.[49] I have distinguished three elements. The first element consists in the Christian community's interpretive judgments (or hermeneutical reconstruction) about the integrity of the tradition and what counts as paradigmatic for the tradition. The second element consists in the retroductive warrants from experiences and praxis. The third consists in background theories, be they scientific, philosophical or ethical. My point has

---

[47] Of his several essays, see especially "Wide Reflective Equilibrium and Theory Acceptance in Ethics," *Journal of Philosophy* 76 (1979) 256–82, and "Two Approaches toward Theory Acceptance in Ethics" in David Copp and David Zimmerman, eds., *Morality, Reason, and Truth* (Totowa, N.J.: Rowman & Allanheld, 1985), 120–40.

[48] Ronald Dworkin, *Law's Empire* (Cambridge: Harvard University, 1986), 176–225.

[49] In addition to *Foundational Theology*, see also "Foundations of Theology: A Community's Tradition of Discourse and Praxis," in George Kilcourse, ed., *Catholic Theology in North American Context* (Macon, GA: Mercer University Press, 1987), 107–34. For a different theological appeal to reflective equilibrium, see Ronald Thiemann, *Revelation and Theology*.

ought
phenomenon been that all three elements are intertwined and interactive; all lead to mutual adjustments.

How the Christian community interprets its tradition affects what a community considers to be a retroductive warrant. It influences how a community interprets contemporary practices and experiences. It also bears upon its interpretation of background conceptions. Likewise, background assumptions as well as retroductive warrants from contemporary experience affect what a community considers to be paradigmatic in its tradition.

Such a broad reflective equilibrium is distinct from a narrow reflective equilibrium. A narrow reflective equilibrium takes place in the interpretation of tradition. A community constantly interprets its tradition in terms of its integrity. When conflicts or inconsistencies emerge, it becomes necessary to reconstruct what is paradigmatic in the tradition. Such reinterpretations seek to achieve the integrity of the overall tradition. For example, in dealing with the issue of the ordination of women, many Christian communities have had to face the fact that many traditions considered women inferior and unequal. Moreover, such traditions have also excluded women from ordained ministry. Yet the traditions also radically affirmed that all are redeemed in Christ.

When such tensions within the traditions come acutely to the fore as conflicts, then the need for integrity and for the resolution of conflicts emerges. The task of reinterpreting and reconstructing the integrity of the tradition becomes an urgent task for the community. Through a reinterpretation of its tradition a community achieves an internal norm that calls for change. Yet it calls for change not only for experience but also for the sake of the integrity of its tradition.

The method of a broad reflective equilibrium explicitly underscores that reinterpretations of the integrity of a religious tradition affect not only an interpretation of contemporary experience, but also background assumptions. The reinterpretation of the tradition is in turn also affected by warrants from contemporary experience and by background theories. No single element is isolated from the process as an independent and exclusive foundation. The goal of theology is to seek a reflective integrity among all the diverse elements and in relation to each element. Broad reflective equilibrium adds background theories and retroductive warrants to narrow reflective equilibrium. It is thereby more critically self-conscious.

Reflective Equilibrium
and Niebuhr's Practice of Theology

Comparee to HRW

Niebuhr's practice of theology, more than his theory of theology, involved a type of reflective equilibrium. An examination of Niebuhr's *de facto* practice of theology will show this. This examination will be guided by asking whether a type of reflective equilibrium is present. Then Niebuhr's conception of the nature of theology will be compared to the method of reflective equilibrium in both recent moral philosophy and foundational theology.

Niebuhr's Type of Reflective Equilibrium

Niebuhr emphasized that Christian theology starts with a set of initial commitments and values. Theology does not abstract from these. It does not start from a position beyond the flow of history and the ebb of society. This emphasis is evident not just in Niebuhr's observations on relativism and his early references to a confessional theology. It is also present in his understanding of theology as a practical reasoning in faith and in his elaboration of the "reflective method" of theology.

In addition, Niebuhr approached the Christian tradition with elements of what I call a "hermeneutical reconstruction." In *The Responsible Self,* he contrasted two alternative patterns of interpretation. One way is the path of anti-traditionalism. Taken by Descartes and radical empiricism, this path starts with radical doubt. It challenges every tradition and received notion. It has worked well in science, for it has allowed scientists to cast aside their anthropomorphic conceptions of the world.[50] Yet such an approach has not been successful in dealing with persons and communities. It reduces persons and communities to objects. The other path, suitable for the area of interpersonal relations, remembers an internal history. This path reorganizes rather than abandons the past. It retrospectively reconstructs in a way similar to analytical psychology.[51]

Niebuhr's ethics must deal with the following problem: God's standpoint is comprehensive and catholic, yet persons have only

---

[50] Niebuhr, *The Responsible Self,* 101–2.
[51] Ibid., 102.

limited, partial and finite standpoints. How then do persons with their limited standpoints know God's universal standpoint? Niebuhr attempted to develop a standpoint as a bridge between human valuations and God's valuations. He approached the problem by critically examining traditional notions of conscience. He related them to George H. Mead's notion of *"impartial* spectator" and *"generalized* other." Niebuhr did not seek simply to gain a social understanding of conscience, but to go beyond it. The self is responsible not simply to the social ethos of groups, but rather to others as Thou's, and not only to the Thou's and the You, but also to that which the Thou and You respond.[52] Niebuhr sought a standpoint that is more than the social conscience of a community—a standpoint against which persons can judge themselves.

Niebuhr's emphasis on initial commitments, his attempt to have a standpoint over against individual judgments, his appeal to the fertility of the symbol of the responsible self, and his development of theocentricism and the universal community are all elements which, taken together, represent a type of reflective equilibrium. These elements point to a reflective equilibrium sensitive to the historical condition of knowledge. Such sensitivity shows a use of reflective equilibrium that is much less rationalist than that of John Rawls. An analysis of Niebuhr's description and practice of theology will display further differences. It will also help answer the question whether a "fitting evaluation" alone characterizes Niebuhr's method.

Niebuhr's Definition and Practice

Niebuhr used diverse terms, e.g., "response," "fitting," "interactional," and "dialogue." Moreover, he used these terms almost synonymously. Nevertheless, it seems to me that there is a significant difference between a response that is fitting and a response that entails interaction and dialogue. The image of a fitting response does not necessarily imply interaction or dialogue. Nor does it necessarily exclude it. Nevertheless, the notion of a fitting response emphasizes the response as a reaction to existing reality, to that which is already given. Interaction and dialogue,

---

[52] See Niebuhr, "The Ego-Alter Dialectic and the Conscience," in *Journal of Philosophy* 42 (1945) 352–59, and *The Responsible Self*, 69–89.

however, emphasize more a constructive dimension. Interaction and dialogue require a back and forth movement. A dialogue does not simply require fitting responses, but gives rise in the dialectic of the conversation to new insights, knowledge, and decisions. Such interactions are at the heart of the mutual adjustments demanded by reflective equilibrium. The notion of a fitting response, in contrast, conjures up the image of a correspondence to a given reality. It suggests the appropriateness of a certain pattern of response. In short, reflective equilibrium is much more constructive and emphasizes criteria of coherence. A fitting response is much more realistic and emphasizes criteria of appropriateness.

Much of what Niebuhr affirmed corresponds to the model of a fitting response. There is a finite and fitting response to God and God's action in the world. Yet much of what Niebuhr declared about theological knowledge and interpretation is also "interactional." His image of the human person as the *homo dialogicus* clearly denotes more than response.[53] Moreover, a fitting response is part of a process of continuing interaction and interpretation. This complementarity in Niebuhr's statements raises a question. Would a method of reflective equilibrium rather than one of fitting valuation more faithfully express his theology?

The distinction between the definition of truth and the criterion of truth can assist our interpretation of Niebuhr's conception.[54] Philosophical analysis often distinguishes the definition from the criterion of truth in order to show that coherence and correspondence theories of truth need not rival each other. A correspondence theory supplies the definition of truth, whereas a coherence theory supplies the criterion of truth. Niebuhr clearly had a realistic definition of truth. Yet I would contend that he employed coherence criteria.

On the one hand, Niebuhr explicitly advocated realism. He appealed to the realism of the scientific ideal of his day. He pointed to the scientific practice of assuming the reality of its object. He argued, therefore, that theology, just like other sciences, must affirm the reality of its object. On the other hand, Niebuhr's

---

[53] Niebuhr, *The Responsible Self*, 57, 160 for the image of *homo dialogicus*.

[54] For the importance of the distinction between a definition of truth and criteria of truth in general, see Susan Haack, *Philosophy of Logics* (Cambridge: Cambridge University Press, 1978), 86–134.

epistemology acknowledged the relativity and historicity of all human valuations and categories. He did not appeal to one set of data as an isolated criterion of truth, for he realized that experience, tradition, and language are conditioned. As a result, he strove to explicate the coherence between monotheistic faith and the interpretation of other values. This double awareness led to a double affirmation. Niebuhr affirmed the objectivity of religious valuation, and he used the language of "fitting response" and "responsible valuation." Yet he also insisted that one determines what is a responsible valuation or a fitting response not simply by taking a look at what is out there. Instead, one must consider a complex interplay of interpretive criteria and valuations.

Reflective Equilibrium Diffs versus Responsible Valuation

A comparison of Niebuhr's concept of responsible valuation with the method of reflective equilibrium reveals several basic differences concerning conceptions of the human self and of method. These basic differences point to differences in criteria, and raise foundational issues affecting the nature of theology.

Conception of Self

Two radically different conceptions of the self are operative in these different approaches. H. Richard Niebuhr had a notion of the self as radically dependent. The self is not simply historically and socially determined, but is radically dependent upon the One, the Creator God. Niebuhr's interpretation of dependency led him to affirm that "it seems truer to say that I am being lived than that I live."[55] Niebuhr, indeed, also stressed human choice and freedom within dependency, in his eloquent conclusion to *Christ and Culture*,[56] for example, and in his view of loyalty as the active side of trust.[57] Yet he understood the self primarily as "patient."[58] There-

---

[55] Niebuhr, *The Responsible Self*, 114.

[56] Niebuhr, *Christ and Culture* (New York: Harper & Row, 1951), 249–56.

[57] Libertus A. Hoedemaker, *The Theology of H. Richard Niebuhr* (Philadelphia: Pilgrim Press, 1970), 70–73.

[58] On this very point, a comparison with Karl Rahner's theology of the self and God would be illuminating. For Rahner, dependency and autonomy were dialecti-

fore, he could trenchantly quip, "men can practice birth-control, but not self-creation."[59]

In contrast, the fulcrum point of Rawls's contract theory is the self as unencumbered and autonomous. The original position, with its veil of ignorance, abstracts individuals from any social and historical particulars, thereby enabling them to decide freely and rationally for the principles of justice that should underlie a just, ordered society. Freedom and autonomy are at the center of such a conception. In advocating the image of the human person as responsible over against the image of the human person as citizen, Niebuhr argued against "the German interpreters in whom the Kantian symbolism holds sway, [for whom] the deontological interpretation of man the obedient legislator has been used not only as the key to Biblical interpretation but for the definition of the true Christian life."[60] These theologians equated the gospel ethos with deontological ethics in terms of an "ethics of obedience" or an ethics of "radical obedience." For Niebuhr, however, the decisive issue was not what is the law to which we must be obedient. The decisive issue was, rather, what is the fitting and responsible response to what is going on, and to what God's intention is in the present.

Niebuhr's criticism concerning the appeal of Barth, Bultmann, and Bonhoeffer to an ethics of obedience was correct. But he was wrong in his critique of Kant and the symbol of the human person as citizen. Kant based moral legislation upon what persons agree to as free and equal rational beings. The principles that persons act upon are not adopted heteronomously out of obedience, but autonomously out a free rational choice. The Kantian categorical imperative applies to persons as free and rational who act on principles that they would chose as independent and rational persons.[61]

---

cally related. The more the human self is related to God, the more the human self achieves its authentic autonomy. It comes, therefore, as no surprise that Latin American liberation theology has much of its intellectual roots in Rahner's theology. This observation raises the question: what type of political theology would stem from Niebuhr's emphasis on the self as patient? Is the critique of liberation theology by one of his students a legitimate consequence of this theology?

[59] Niebuhr, *The Responsible Self*, 115.

[60] Ibid., 66.

[61] Rawls, *Theory of Justice*, 251, and his Dewey Lectures, "Kantian Constructivism in Moral Theory," *Journal of Philosophy* 77 (1980) 515–72.

These differences from Kant profile Niebuhr's legacy. Today, criticisms of the liberal conception of the self are widespread. Communitarians and feminists argue that the liberal conception falsely assumes the existence of an autonomous and unencumbered self.[62] Niebuhr's analysis of the self pointed to multiple relations. The self relates to nature, to others, to society, and to a cause. His vision of the self went beyond the liberal conception. His interpretation of the self as "patient" is an image he appropriated to deal with suffering and war.[63] But is this image adequate to the constructive task of legislating a just society that corrects existing patterns of discrimination? Is this image adequate for nations seeking to develop principles of international justice among nations of unequal power and resources? Is it adequate for the liberation of women who have been told to be "patient"?

How does one answer these questions? The responsible decision for the Kantian deontological position means adherence to those principles of justice that we freely chose as rational. The responsible decision for Niebuhr was a response based on our knowledge of what is going on, based on our recognition of God's intention in the present historical situation. Yet the decisive issue remains: How does one know? How does the Kantian know what rationally free persons would choose? How did Niebuhr know what God's intention was? The questions of method and criteria become decisive.

Differences of Method

One might characterize the differences between a method of reflective equilibrium and an ethics of responsibility in terms of a naturalistic versus a non-naturalistic approach, or in terms of a realistic versus a constructive approach to truth and goodness. But such a response is too simple.

---

[62] For a survey, see Amy Gutmann, "Communitarian Critics of Liberalism," *Philosophy and Public Affairs* 14 (1985) 308–22 and Christopher Lasch, "The Communitarian Critique of Liberalism," *Soundings* 69 (1986) 60–76. Susan Okin, Seyla Benhabib, Iris Young, and Nancy Frazer attempt to bring feminism into relation with Rawls (and, for the last three, with Habermas). See Seyla Benhabib, ed., *Feminism as Critique* (Minneapolis: University of Minnesota Press, 1987) and Susan Moller Okin, "Justice and Gender," *Philosophy and Public Affairs* 16 (1987) 42–72.

[63] See the important and careful analysis by Richard B. Miller, "H. Richard Niebuhr's War Articles: A Transvaluation of Value," *Journal of Religion* 68 (1988) 242–62.

Another approach to this question relates Niebuhr's ethics to theories of meta-ethics. C. David Grant takes this approach and classifies Niebuhr's ethics as "naturalism." "It is not alien to Niebuhr's thought," he argues, "to see value as a 'property' ascribable to beings simply considered."[64] Niebuhr did not consider "fittingness" primarily as a psychological state, such as pleasantness. Instead, "fittingness" is objective and realistic. It refers to the "apprehended quality of relations between beings."[65]

I would prefer not to pigeonhole Niebuhr's ethical stance in terms of what G. E. Moore called the "naturalistic fallacy."[66] The naturalistic fallacy viewed goodness as a natural property or as an apprehended quality. Niebuhr's position, in my opinion, was not simply naturalistic. For Niebuhr, as for Kierkegaard, the moral quality of good was not simply a predicate quality, but was, rather, the agent's total being in action. The value of individual beings stands in relation not only to other beings, but also to what is specified as the center of value. Niebuhr recognized that empirical experiences take place within the context of interpretation, and that patterns of interpretation affect our experience of nature, of others, and of events. All of these influence the interpretation given to alteration and to the specification of fittingness.

The label "naturalism" raises the problem of objectivity and realism. Niebuhr argued that realism and objectivity are the characteristic features of twentieth-century theology.[67] These features contrast with the idealism and psychologism of nineteenth-century theology. Moreover, they define theology's goal. "The task of theology is neither the systematization of authoritative material nor the description of religious consciousness but the definition of that stratum of reality which religion intends."[68] This task challenges the theologian "to discover that methodology which will lead theology and the philosophy of religion to a precise definition of the religious object."[69]

Niebuhr never ceased to affirm this objectivity and realism. Yet

---

[64] C. David Grant, *God the Center of Value*, 89.

[65] Ibid., 90.

[66] G. E. Moore, *Principia Ethica* (Cambridge: Cambridge University Press, 1903).

[67] See Niebuhr, "Religious Realism in the Twentieth Century," in D. C. Mcintosh, ed., *Religious Realism* (New York: Macmillan Co., 1931), 413–28.

[68] Ibid., 423.

[69] Ibid., 425–26.

his moral philosophy did not appeal to naturalistic intuitions or perceptive apprehensions of goodness. Instead, it appealed to the proper relation between individual valuation and the center of value. His stress on objectivity and realism served as an affirmation that religion is about God and not about religious subjectivity. Morality is about the responsible valuation of the fitting response in relation to goodness and rightness. God and goodness are not illusions or even delusions.

A different conception of objectivity is possible. Moral objectivity relates also to public discourse, and in a way that correlates objectivity and constructivity.[70] "What justifies a conception of justice is not its being true to an order antecedent to and given to us, but its congruence with our deeper understanding of ourselves and our aspirations, and our realization that given our history and the traditions embedded in our public life, it is the most reasonable doctrine for us . . . Kantian constructivism holds that moral objectivity is to be understood in terms of a suitably constructed social point of view that all can accept."[71] This constructivism serves as an argument for reflective equilibrium as a method employing public moral discourse as a condition.

This conception of moral principles as constructive differs from an ethics based on value theory or on responsible evaluation with regard to the definition and criteria of truth. A method of broad reflective equilibrium does not contain only coherence criteria of truth,[72] even though its definition of truth itself does not equate objectivity with naturalism and realism in the same way the other theories do.[73] Instead, conditions of public discourse become essential as required conditions under which consensus and agreement should be reached. Public discourse and consensus enter into the conditions of justification. Realism is involved in background theory and in reference to practical consequences. However, its role is subordinate to public consensus and to the construction of the

[70] See John Rawls's Dewey Lectures, especially the third lecture, "Construction and Objectivity," 554–72.

[71] Rawls, Dewey Lectures, 519.

[72] For constraints on a coherence theory of truth, see Fiorenza, "Foundations of Theology: A Community's Tradition of Discourse and Praxis," 118–21.

[73] On this point Jürgen Habermas's distinction among the propositional, intelligible, normative, and expressive offers a much more nuanced conception. Definitions of truth should take into account all these elements.

principles of justice. Is such a constructivism based primarily on free public consensus suitable for theology, or is the realism of a fitting response more suitable for theology? The answer is not simple.

Particularity and Universality in Theology

A comparison of Niebuhr's understanding of a fitting valuation with a contemporary theory of reflective equilibrium underscores this question. Much within Niebuhr's theology allowed for elements of a reflective equilibrium: his starting point from the concrete valuation of faith, his holism, the catholicity of his criteria, and the interrelation between theory and practice. Nevertheless, decisive for his understanding of the self and of theological method is the appeal to the "fittingness" of a response in faith to God, and his critique of any theology centered on valuations outside of this faith relation.

This difference provides points of comparison between the approach of fitting valuation and a method of reflective equilibrium. An analysis of these comparisons in relation to those issues raised at the beginning of this essay shows H. Richard Niebuhr's relevance for theology today: the critique of foundationalism, relativism, communities of interpretation, and theory and practice.

Critique of Foundationalism and the Foundation of Theology

Although Niebuhr's theology displayed diverse approaches and starting points, on one point he was adamant. One should not make relative human values the starting-point of theology, as previous theologies of value have. "They assume," he argued, "that humans have a knowledge of absolutely valid values which is not only independent of their knowledge of God but which is also in some way determinative of God."[74] His philosophical arguments against these theologies of value constituted an impressive critique of foundationalism. His critique of liberal theology within this quotation

---

[74] Niebuhr, "Value Theory and Theology," in Julius Seelye Bixler et al., eds., *The Nature of Religious Experience: Essays in Honor of Douglas Clyde Macintosh* (New York: Harper & Brothers, 1937), 95. See the response by D. C. Macintosh, "Theology, Valuation or Existential?", *Review of Religion* 4 (1939) 23–44.

contains three points of contention: [1] the knowledge of absolutely valid value judgments; [2] the possibility of knowing these values independently of one's knowledge of God; and [3] the establishment of these values as determinative of God.

A method of reflective equilibrium enables one to appropriate Niebuhr's basic insight into religious knowledge as well as his critique of an epistemological foundationalism, and yet bypass the conflict with liberal theology. A theology seeking a broad reflective integrity or equilibrium acknowledges the hypothetical character of one's considered judgments and valuations, and the historic character of traditions. It also acknowledges, however, the relative character of one's background theories about personhood and goodness, and the tentativeness of retroductive warrants from practice.

Such a theology does not view the problem as Niebuhr saw it. It does not advocate a secure knowledge of absolutely valid values. One makes considered judgments within the context of tradition, society, and praxis. Those judgments and principles are constantly subject to testing and revising. Even our deepest acts of trust, loyalty, and confidence are finite, intrinsically embedded in the finite and relative categories that express them. The ultimate object of our most fundamental trust is conceptualized in categories. These categories are open to revision because of the very transcendence of ultimacy and the contingency of our language.

Many philosophers seek to establish the logical independence of ethics from religion.[75] Theologians who are sensitive to the location of all reflection within a cultural and religious tradition argue that our conceptions of goodness are not independent from historical religious traditions. Rather, they argue that our historically conditioned conceptions of God and goodness are correlative. Our conceptions of the good do not simply determine our conceptions of God. Theological reflection is such that the conception of God and the conception of the good are correlatively interpreted and reconstructed. Niebuhr's critique of foundationalism was valid and should be affirmed. Nevertheless, the liberal attempt to have language about God and ethical language exercise a mutually critical influence also remains.

[75] For a critique of this position, see Jeffrey Stout, *Ethics after Babel: The Languages of Morals and Their Discontents* (Boston: Beacon Press, 1988).

66   *Francis Schüssler Fiorenza*

Relativism: Objectivity as Integrity and Publicness

The critique of foundationalism leads most directly to the issue of
relativism. Niebuhr resolved the issue of relativism by insisting not
only that religious knowledge is relational, but also that knowledge
of God is present only within a relational valuation. Does this
answer cohere with relativism and with the awareness of the conditioned and constructive character of all human knowledge?

Niebuhr's answer combined coherence and realism. He acknowledged change, but only limited change. Personal reinterpretations and social reconstructions take place, yet they do not radically change the general pattern of response, for they do not revise
the sense of the ultimate context.[76] Reinterpretations of the past do
lead to new understandings of the past. Yet despite his acknowledgment of the historicity of all interpretations, Niebuhr
affirmed an objectivist permanency in regard to the sense of the
ultimate.

The example of the Christian belief in creation, when read from
the perspective of a method of reflective equilibrium, can illustrate
my point as well as Niebuhr's. The Christian community's belief
in creation involves the interpretation of tradition, background
theories, and warrants from experience. The Christian interpretation of the Bible may view the creation accounts not simply as an
explication of the human experience of finitude. It may also view
them as an exposition of a belief in God's creation in six days and in
God's special creation of humans within a hierarchical order of
creation. This view might be intertwined with background theories
heavily indebted to Aristotelian physics and biology. This view
might also be intertwined with the societal experience of a highly
structured and ordered society. All of these come together to form
a reflective equilibrium and to give content to the belief in creation.

This traditional equilibrium, however, becomes shattered. Background theories from biology and from astronomy demolish the
Aristotelian worldview. Political revolutions invalidate the experience of society as ordered by divine will. Historical criticisms and
analyses undo the traditional interpretation of the biblical accounts
of creation. The result is a crisis of faith and a challenge to theological reflection.

[76] Niebuhr, *The Responsible Self*, 106.

The challenge to theological reflection is to construct a new formulation of the Christian belief in God's creation. Theologians attempting a creative new formulation of the Christian belief have to seek a new equilibrium that takes into account scientific background theories, new experiences of equality rather than hierarchy in society, and new interpretations of biblical texts as well as new readings of the non-literal interpretations of creation by classical church writers.

In the face of this shattering of many elements of traditional religious knowledge, theological reflection needs to reconstruct religious belief and to reinterpret its religious tradition. Yet despite all the new imput—from scientific background theories, for example—one does not go back to astronomy. One does not learn the religious meaning of creation, for example, by reading Steven Weinberg's *The First Three Minutes*,[77] or by listening to the latest debates about whether the universe is a string or a bubble. On this point H. Richard Niebuhr was correct. This remains his legacy for us, a legacy that he handed down to us from Schleiermacher and Ritschl (*pace* neo-orthodox historiography).

Yet the very categories, concepts, and even, in part, the experience of the meaning of creation have changed radically. I now experience createdness as equality before ultimacy. Previously, others might have experienced it as inequality before ultimacy. Religious valuations and experiences are radically interpretive, and thereby permeated with human constructive categories. Wittgenstein's critique of private experience and language has had a decisive influence. As a result, many contemporary theologians would underscore this very point. They would emphasize much more strongly than Niebuhr did the degree to which all religious experience is interpretive and linguistic.[78] Therefore there is not a sense of ultimacy underlying changing conceptions of ultimacy.

Changing conceptions of ultimacy are intertwined with the experience of ultimacy. Faith in God as the center of value is therefore intertwined with changing conceptions of God. For this

[77] Steven Weinberg, *The First Three Minutes* (New York: Basic Books, 1977).

[78] This same point has been made recently from two different philosophical and theological perspectives: George Lindbeck, *The Nature of Doctrine* (Philadelphia: Westminster Press,1984) and Wayne Proudfoot, *Religious Experience* (Berkeley: University of California Press, 1985).

reason, a method of broad reflective equilibrium is needed to complement Niebuhr's reflective method and his emphasis on responsible valuation. Such a reflective equilibrium does not deny that Christian faith has God as the center of its value. Nor does a method of reflective equilibrium deny that Christian theology as a theology must reflect on this faith in relation to God as its center of value. Rather, it insists that such faith and valuation are intertwined with concepts, interpretations, and background theories that need to be critically examined so that Christian faith can be critically reflective and self-conscious.

My proposal acknowledges Niebuhr's insight into the significance of religious valuation, for knowledge is a legacy that we should not neglect. Yet it places those elements of coherence and comprehensiveness in his practice of theology much more strongly at the forefront than his emphasis on realism allows him.

Christian Community and Rationality

Since this point involves a central disagreement, it needs further explication. An example can profile the disagreement and relate it to the issues of communities of public discourse and rationality. Take, for example, the question: Is God just? Niebuhr's realism asserted that God is really just. Therefore the question should not be equated with a question such as: Is butter pecan or French vanilla a more tasteful ice cream? Moreover, if one pointed out the different ideas of justice, Niebuhr would affirm that despite these differences, the basic religious trust that the ultimate reality is loving and just exhibits a permanence of truth and valuation. This permanence of valuation would underlie all these different categories of justice.

I am not so sure. If, however, one's basic ideas of justice were gathered from Robert Nozick's individualistic entitlement theory, then one's basic religious experience of reality as ultimately loving and just would be that one is entitled to all one's achievements.[79] After all, God's love and valuation manifest themselves in the industriousness and righteousness of those he loves. If one's basic

---

[79] Robert Nozick, *Anarchy, State, and Utopia* (New York: Basic Books, 1983), especially Part II.

ideas of justice followed John Rawls's "difference principle" (which within limits focuses on the rights of the disadvantaged), then one's basic experience of reality as ultimately loving and just would be an experience not so much of entitlement as of commitment to the disadvantaged and to the option for the poor.

Such considerations should lead us to test our religious experiences and valuations. They should be tested not only in free and public discourse within one's religious community and in relation to one's religious tradition, but also in relation to background theories about society as well as to ethical public discourse. This public discourse and this reflective testing of experience, tradition, and background theories provide the conditions for a reflective method encouraging a self-critical faith that acknowledges its relativity.

At the same time, this appeal to relate one's religious convictions, experiences, and values to public discourse must be sensitive to the critique of foundationalism, in the way that theology was. A theology sensitive to this critique cannot understand the criterion of public discourse as a universal, common, or neutral public, as if theology could search for a universal starting point like Rawls's original position, or as if theology could appeal to a common human experience.[80] Instead, Christian theology is reflection on a concrete faith of a particular historical community.

On this point, advocates of public theology can learn from Niebuhr. Often they want to appeal to universal criteria, common to everyone.[81] They argue that theology should speak to common human experience, even secular experience. Such an approach is like someone who is trying to reach diverse groups and decides to speak Esperanto. Then she congratulates herself that she has indeed communicated with everyone within the universal community of humankind because she has spoken a universal

---

[80] For an attempt to relate a more universalistic position, represented by Rawls and Habermas, to a position seeking to interpret a normative tradition, see Francis Schüssler Fiorenza, "Politische Theologie und liberale Gerechtigkeitskonzeptionen," in Eduard Schillebeeckx, ed., *Mystik und Politik* (Mainz: Matthias-Grünewald, 1988), 95–104, and Fiorenza, "Die Kirche als Interpretationsgemeinschaft. Politische Theologie zwischen Diskursethik und hermeneutischer Rekonstruktion," in Edmund Arens, ed., *Habermas und die Theologie* (Dusseldorf: Patmos, 1989), 115–44.

[81] See my critique of the appeal to common human experience, *Foundational Theology*, 276–84.

language. But in fact no one group or nation speaks Esperanto, even though Esperanto is constructed to be a universal language.

Theology, spoken in the key of a universal language, is spoken in a key to which all persons are not attuned. Here is the relevance of Niebuhr's so-called "confessional approach." Niebuhr was aware that knowledge of God takes place in practical trust. This knowledge of God, morever, becomes crystallized in the internal history and stories of particular historical religious communities. Thus, individual community with its internal history interacts with other overlapping communities. Public discourse is, therefore, important not simply as an expressive move toward other communities. It contributes to the genuine mutual adjustment and self-critique of our internal stories that can take place.

Niebuhr's own practice of theology strove toward a universality and publicness that I am advocating. Niebuhr wrote that Christianity "understands that faith in God cannot become incarnate except in a universal community in which all walls of partition have been broken down . . . The drive to universality has been present in Christianity from the beginning; it has been expressed in its expansive and missionary movements as well as in its efforts to maintain a catholic church."[82]

Conclusion

In this essay I have argued that H. R. Niebuhr's theology was sensitive to the issues raised by the critique of foundationalism, namely, lack of secure foundations for knowledge and belief, the relativity of human knowledge and values, the interpretive role of communities, and the interrelation between theory and practice. This sensitivity influenced his understanding of the nature and criteria of Christian theology. His theological appropriation of value theory enabled him to takes seriously these foundational issues without falling into either objectivism or relativism.

In this context the notion of responsible valuation was central. It provided the link between Christian theology and ethics. In his moral theory, the responsible valuation consisted of an interpretive fitting response to the world and God's action in the world. In Christian theology, responsible valuation took the form of reflective

[82] Niebuhr, *Radical Monotheism*, 62.

method upon the triadic structure of faith. This responsible valuation expressed itself in a critique of henotheism and polytheism, and in an affirmation of radical faith in God as the center of value.

Since value theory, borrowed from philosophical and ethical theory, provided an important basis for Niebuhr's method, it was compared with the current use of the method of reflective equilibrium. The end result of this comparison was my suggestion that Niebuhr's method had the advantage of focusing on the priority of the valuation of God as the center of values. The method of reflective equilibrium has the advantage of underscoring that valuations take place with diverse interpretation, ideas, practices, and background theories, mutually correcting each other. These remarks are not meant to criticize Niebuhr, but rather to show the significance and legacy of his work for the theological task today.

I have maintained that Christian theology should appropriate a method of broad reflective equilibrium that tries to take into account Niebuhr's key insights. In doing so, I am aware of a warning Niebuhr expressed. In an early essay Niebuhr lumped together liberal Protestant theologians and Roman Catholic Thomists. Both seek to define a unified system of value, yet both, he lamented, start from below, from particular values, and then try to ascend to God.[83] My proposal of a broad reflective equilibrium as a theological method seeks to avoid that danger. It strives to be faithful to Niebuhr's critique. It takes as its starting point the considered judgments of the Christian community about the integrity of its tradition. It relates those judgments with background theories and retroductive warrants from experience. It seeks, thereby, to bring those judgments in relation to human rationality and public discourse about justice for the universal human community. The priority given to religious judgments, the emphasis on community, the critique of absolutizing relative standpoints, and the loyalty to a cause and to a universal community are insights about which all Christian theologians still have much to learn from H. Richard Niebuhr.[84]

---

[83] Niebuhr, "Value Theory," 108.

[84] For stylistic and editorial suggestions, I am grateful to my research assistant, Sara McClintock.

4

Response to Francis Schüssler Fiorenza

James M. Gustafson

The structure of Professor Fiorenza's paper suggests three foci of attention: his interpretation of Niebuhr; his critique of Niebuhr; and his proposal for theology and ethics as that is related to Niebuhr. But before I turn to those, I want to make a few trifling remarks:

1. In relation to Fiorenza's note on Donald Fadner about whether Niebuhr had a view of common human experience, I wonder what Fiorenza does with "All life has the character of responsiveness, I maintain" (*The Responsible Self*, 46).
2. Fiorenza indicates that Niebuhr took account of the philosophical insight into the socially conditioned character of knowledge. There are anticipations of that in history, e.g., Francis Bacon's idols of tribe, cave, marketplace and theatre in *Novum Organum*. The insight might be philosophical, but my impression is that for persons like Niebuhr it comes from a sociological and historical perspective. We skew Niebuhr if we fail to consider the extent of his reading in classic sociological literature.
3. Fiorenza notes a tendency to interpret Niebuhr more in relation to European background than American. I only note that this

judgment depends on what dissertations, papers and articles one reads. William Spohn's paper for this symposium ("The Ethics of the Fitting in the American Speculative Tradition") is only one of several that would provide counter-evidence.

*title
07
Spohn*

I take the fundamental structure of the paper to be shaped by the polarity between particularity and universality. Maybe the anti-foundationalism/foundationalism polarity points to the same principal issue. It takes nothing away from Fiorenza's accolades to Niebuhr's prescience to wonder whether the issue on which these polarities rest is not a very old one that takes on different terminology in different generations of thinkers. With the publication of *Faith on Earth*, there is even stronger public evidence of Niebuhr's fruitful thinking on issues.

Fiorenza's Interpretation of Niebuhr

Here I isolate four points:

1. Fiorenza's discussion of Niebuhr's use of the term disinterestedness seems to me to involve an overinterpretation. Given various contexts in which the term is used, I do not find the use to be as problematic as does Fiorenza. But Fiorenza's own suggestion of "theocentric interestedness" seems to me to be worthy of consideration, at least for some contexts in Niebuhr's work.

2. I think Fiorenza has skewed Niebuhr significantly. Note, for example, his summary sentence, "the primary purpose of *theology* is the intellectual love of God and neighbor." I find no warrants for this in Niebuhr, nor in the citations Fiorenza uses. Niebuhr wrote that "no substitute can be found for the definition of the *goal* of the *Church* [not theology—emphases added] as the *increase among men of the love of God and neighbor*" (*The Purpose of the Church and its Ministry* [1956], 31). The purpose of the church cannot be equated with the purpose of theology. Theology is an intellectual activity in the service of the church's purpose. I know of no texts which warrant the stress Fiorenza places on intellectual love of God. Theology is intellectual activity; one might say it has a context in love for God, but the use of "intellectual" to modify love skews Niebuhr's view of theology.

3. Fiorenza worries about where Niebuhr "starts out." Odd as it seems to use " starting out" in this context, I think Niebuhr

started out from several places—always at least three—at once. Fiorenza notes the significance of the well-known triadic structure, but I think he fails to grasp its implications for "starting out." He says Niebuhr did not " start out" from human experience, yet there is the sentence I quoted, that "all life has the character of responsiveness." Perhaps that is a statement of what Edward Farley, with reference to another theologian, called "the common sense ontology." I am not persuaded, as Fiorenza is, that Niebuhr "starts out" from the concrete particular to show how it is related to the universal. The conviction of the universal is there also "from the beginning." Maybe Fiorenza's language of "starting out" is ill-considered, or perhaps I am confused. In neither the sense of fundamental assumption nor the sense of temporality do I find his case persuasive.

4. The gravest problem I have with Fiorenza's interpretation of Niebuhr is that he does not expound Niebuhr's theology, i.e., his interpretations of God, God's relation to human beings, nature, history and society, the significance of Christ for Christians, etc. I always have difficulties with studies of methods of investigation that are not integrated with the object of investigation. I could interpret Niebuhr quite fairly to make an argument that the object of theological investigation, God, has to be taken into account in the development of method. Indeed, the triad requires this.

Niebuhr said some very powerful things about God, and some things are in tension with each other, as they are in much of Western theology. The way in which he wrote about God was related to particular contexts; as the context changed the emphasis changed. For example, there is the theological voluntarism in that startling claim that "God is acting in all actions upon you" (*The Responsible Self*, 126). This coheres with aspects of his ethics—responding to God's action upon us. The method of responsiveness in ethics is, perhaps, as much a matter of seeing the ethical significance of that theological conviction as it is a matter of defining a type of ethics distinct from other historical types.

I cannot grasp Niebuhr's faith and religion, his theology and his ethics, and his theological and ethical method without positing that theological conviction. The voluntarism is in some tension with the writing about Being, and The One Beyond the Many. Take, for example, sentences from the 1957 Montgomery Lectures (*Radical Monotheism and Western Culture*); the context—theological lectures in a secular university—might have affected what he said and how he said it: "Radical monotheism dethrones all absolutes short of the principle of being itself. At the same time it reverences every relative existent. Its two great mottoes are: 'I am the Lord thy God; thou shalt have no other gods before me' and 'Whatever is, is good.'" (*Radical Monotheism*, 37).

These sentences are about God and God's creation, and the form and method of those lectures cannot, in my judgment, be understood without grasping and taking into account the reality of God posited in these sentences. I believe, and I think Niebuhr believed, that theology is not altogether different from other "scientific" investigations; insight and intuition informed by traditions and other things lead to positing the character of the reality under investigation. That positing in turn affects the development of methods appropriate to investigation. I think we do not get a fair picture of Niebuhr's methods in theology and ethics without an exposition of the content of his theology.

Fiorenza's Critique of Niebuhr

Fiorenza helps the reader of his paper who might not know his book *Foundational Theology: Jesus and the Church* (1984) and other relevant writings by providing a synopsis of his revision of John Rawls's reflective equilibrium. This becomes a good heuristic device for his assessment of Niebuhr. I shall address two matters in this critique:

1. I think Fiorenza creates a problem in Niebuhr's work that is not really there when he notes a significant difference between a response that is "fitting and one that entails interaction and dialogue." Fiorenza does not distinguish the various contexts in Niebuhr's work in which these (and other) ideas are developed. My interpretation is that interaction and dialogue are more comprehensive in temporal and "spatial" dimensions than is the fitting; the fitting is a moment in continued interaction. Fiorenza himself notes Niebuhr's conception of how the fitting response is in turn responded to, i.e., will be part of the process of continuing interaction and interpretation.

I also think the idea of the fitting is used only in the context of moral action. Richard Crouter has pointed out the Stoic usage of *kathekonta*; most recently Albert Jonsen and Stephen Toulmin, in *The Abuse of Casuistry* (1988), elucidate this in their discussion of the Middle Stoics. Niebuhr's fitting response is to a particular interpreted set of circumstances, time-related, which affects the interaction processes that are its sequilae. (I think interpreters of Niebuhr often do not attend to the particular context in which ideas are developed; like a classic rhetorician, he took that into account.)

2. Fiorenza raises the issue of "patience" in Niebuhr's ethics, an issue raised by other critics as well. In addition to the sentence Fiorenza quotes about being lived more than living, Niebuhr often recalled a sentence from Luther's Table Talk: "I am more acted upon than acting." Niebuhr was, in my judgment, more interested in a true, or at least adequate, description of human experience and reality when he stressed such themes, than in the moral implications of a statement, or the ethical inferences to be drawn from it. The deep sense of dependence on factors beyond human control, the interpretation of actions in relation to events that framed both the limits and possibilities of action—these were matters of description. They were descriptive premises within which discussions of ethics occurred. (Perhaps those of us who come to theology with a heavy dose of the social and natural sciences are more impressed with such interpretations of reality than persons who come from other places.)

I trivialize with examples. I suspect that many, or most of the decisive aspects of Fiorenza's and my life are deeply conditioned, if not determined, by events in which our choice and action was nil or limited (e.g., his Catholicism and my Protestantism), though we have both affirmed what we were born into. I do not know how the Professors Schüssler-Fiorenza chose to marry each other, but in my case I did not autonomously determine the criteria for an appropriate marriage partner and then seek the best candidate. We consent to such conditions, which is different from resignation.

When one remembers, for example, the sentence about God acting in all actions upon us, and the indications of Niebuhr's deep convictions about the sovereign power of God, the ethics cohere not only with a description of experience but also with a theological conviction—and the conviction is backed by the interpretation of

experience. I think that for Niebuhr theology was the most fundamental science, and ethics was second to that. What he believed to
be the truth about God and God's relations set the context for the
ethics. If that led to "patience," so be it. But clearly response also
involves action; it is not passive resignation to events and circumstances.

Fiorenza on Theology and Ethics in Relation to Niebuhr

Here I do not address questions as specific as those I raised in the
two previous sections of this response, but instead offer reflections
on the polarity Fiorenza introduced between particularity and
universality, on reflective equilibrium and its kin, on the criterion of
publicness, etc.

The perceived reality out of which many discussions of Christian
theology and ethics come is, to use a word I normally eschew, pluralism. Christianity has a particular history, and a lot of its theology
and ethics have been caught in a wide or a tight circularity. This
makes it difficult, if not impossible, for Christian apologists or ethicists to participate in "public discourse," or to render their convictions intelligible to those outside the circle. There are circles which
have different centers and seldom overlap within the Christian
community, of which I have become more aware in watching for
the first time in my life some hours of religious telecasting. Two
very different responses can be made to this problem: to accent
Christianity's uniqueness or at least distinctiveness—its particularity, to use the term Fiorenza introduced in his paper; or to seek
some criteria of universality which Christians share, or can share,
with others.

My former colleagues in Chicago have taken great interest in
"public discourse" or "publicness" (to use Fiorenza's term), and
the discussions are widespread in the Christian world. I have
always had difficulties with some ways in which this concern is
stated. My experience and sociological predilections lead me to
observe that there are many publics, and within identifiable publics
there are also various sub-publics. Different publics have different
criteria for truth or adequacy claims. For example, the great Harvard evolutionary theorist and naturalist, Ernst Mayr, in his recent
collection of essays (*Toward a New Philosophy of Biology: Observations
of an Evolutionist*, 1988), makes it clear that biologists think dif-

ferently from physicists and mathematicians (on this it is instructive to read Stephen Hawking's *A Brief History of Time* together with Mayr), and that among paleontologists and biologists there continue to be significant disagreements even after the development of what Mayr calls "the evolutionary synthesis."

So there is no scientific public, except perhaps on very, very generalized or abstract grounds. (More theologians respond to philosophy of science than to particular sciences.) Wayne Booth, in his Ryerson Lecture at the University of Chicago in 1986, brilliantly pointed out the difficulties we have in universities understanding each other's work, not to mention attempting to engage in discourse with one another. Theology is not the only discipline with particular assumptions and difficulties in "public discourse."

My further, perhaps sardonic, observation is that when Christian theologians and ethicists speak of the public, they often have in mind a selected person who, in my judgment, hardly represents inclusive collectivities of scholars, not to mention others. David Tracy, for example, in his book *The Analogical Imagination* (1981), attends in some detail to Marx, Nietzsche and Freud—a public representing certain intellectuals—but does not mention Charles Darwin. My impression is that among my colleagues in ethics the public is often represented by John Rawls, Alan Gewirth, Alasdair MacIntyre, and perhaps a few other philosophers. My experience is that Gewirth's ethical rationalism, for example, is as mysterious to physicians, public policy makers, and private sector policy makers as anything written by a theologian.

My questions at this point are: who is the public whose criteria we are to use? At what level of generality or specificity are we looking for criteria? We ought not, any of us, to contradict ourselves, but how much more specific ought we to be? A colleague told me once that he was getting interested in technology. I asked who he was reading. "Heidegger and Tillich," he replied. I told him he should go beyond them and read something of the history of mining, or communications, or modern agriculture. Heidegger and Tillich hardly represent the technological public. Perhaps methods have to be those of reflective equilibria, not equilibrium, depending on what public we have in mind.

Then there is also the great malleability of the Christian tradition. Fiorenza differentiates between the weights put on various considerations by persons within the spectrum of equilibrium theologians. Douglas J. Hall's *Imaging God: Dominion as Stewardship* (1986) may represent something Fiorenza would find excessive; I do not know. Hall, in his chapter on *imago dei* says that "historical circumstances require us to rethink the fundamentals of our tradition." It sounds radical. What Hall does, put too briefly, is find in the biblical doctrine of the *imago* a view of humans as interrelated with each other and with the natural world. He recognizes that historically this has not been a prominent interpretation, but the seeds were there only to sprout with the environmental crisis. Gordon Kaufman, in one of his early articles, found the *imago* to be man's historicity; others find it to be capacities for rationality, etc. With such malleability I suspect that theologians will always bring tradition into equilibrium with most other considerations.

Something like reflective equilibrium probably went on in Christian theology at least since the time of the Apologists. And something like it has gone on in the development of other intellectual disciplines as well. Toulmin, for example, writes about evolutionary development of disciplines. There are quite a few things in the theological waste disposal that have gotten there either through conscious discarding or simply by atrophying from disuse.

The desire for publicness is certainly fruitful to goad theology and theological ethics from the isolation of insularity. I hope that its proponents will find time to engage in serious discourse with some more specific publics—for example, with economists, politicians (and not just political theorists) et al.—in order to go beyond the abstractions and generalizations of methodological concerns. That experience might affect their methods.

It is one thing to describe the reality or particularity, and another to affirm it normatively. Some of what passes as its defense is simply a descriptive interpretation of certain virtual inevitabilities. Indeed, some of it is similar to what I used to call sociology of religion, not theology or theological method. Where the normative character of the particularity of a Christian way to construe the world, and the beliefs that guide it, has been backed by an articulated and strongly defended doctrine of historical revelation in the events and people of the Bible, there is a truth claim that one can address.

We all know, I think, what we have to do to come to grips with Karl Barth's theology. The particularity there is not the inevitability of partiality or perspectivism on descriptive interpretive grounds, as I think Niebuhr's view of "particularity" was. (Memorable words of Wilhelm Pauck come to mind from his perorations to his lectures on theology since Kant; Troeltsch, not Barth, is the figure that theologians of my generation will have to come to grips with.) I will go no farther on these points. I previously rendered an account of my judgments about the current emphasis on particularism in a published lecture which, I am happy to say, Fiorenza liked.

I spent three of my adolescent years in a village in Kansas. A pastime that required extraordinary skill and/or luck was taking an old Model A Ford out in a pasture. Two boys would sit on the front fenders while a third drove. Each one on the fenders had a single-shot 22. The point was to try to kill a jackrabbit with a single-shot rifle while riding on the fender of a Model A going over a rough pasture. It was hard to find equilibrium with everything moving.

For Niebuhr the center of gravity was God—Being and Actor, briefly mentioned above. Some things, but not all, were moving. A fixed confessional point was stated, among other places, in *The Responsible Self* (1963). I quote only a nub of it. For Christians Jesus Christ "turns their reasoning around so that they do not begin with the premise of God's indifference but of his affirmation of the creature, so that the *Gestalt* which they bring to their experiences of suffering as well as joy, of death as well as of life, is the *Gestalt*, the symbolic form, of grace" (175–76). As circumspect discussions in the lectures *Faith on Earth* show, this affirmation was not made trivially or easily in the light of much experience. If God was *not* the point of equilibrium, God was one of a few clustered points that held Niebuhr's theology steady.

But I respond more generally to various reflective equilibrum-like proposals. If we are in a constant process of adjusting considerations—in Fiorenza's case the hermeneutical reconstruction of what is integral and paradigmatic to the tradition, the retroductive warrants from experience and praxis, and background theories from science, philosophy and ethics—can there ever be anything which decisively compels us to say that the tradition, in its paradigmatic elements, is wrong?

Fiorenza and Niebuhr are both broader in what they will take into account than radically confessional, particularistic theologians, and neither is a universalizing rationalist. But if we give up the criterion of truth claims, particularly correspondence claims, or if we excessively qualify them with a set of coherence claims, Christian theology and ethics might become like trying to shoot a jackrabbit with a single-shot 22, sitting on the fender of a Model A Ford riding through a Kansas pasture. For all of its problems, the criterion barbarously called "publicness" will help to keep us honest, at least. To this university-oriented theologian, it is far more preferable than radical particularism.

5

The Historical Legacy
of H. Richard Niebuhr

Harry S. Stout

As a Christian intellectual who defined himself primarily as a theologian and ethicist, H. Richard Niebuhr had little to do with the classic stuff of which historians' careers are generally made. There are few traces of archival research or edited documents in his publications, no biographies, no articles in American history journals, and no offices in the professional associations. Yet in two books, *The Social Sources of Denominationalism* (1929) and *The Kingdom of God in America* (1937), he produced great histories of American Protestantism that were destined to stand as classics in American historiography. I would like to explore some of the main themes in these works, and suggest why they exerted such a profound influence on the history profession.

Niebuhr's interest in America's religious past was autobiographical as much as it was theoretical. As an immigrant pastor's son growing up in the German-speaking Evangelical Synod, he absorbed a sense of the rich diversity of American religious life and its close connection to ethnic, cultural, and economic factors. This conviction was reinforced by his study of Ernest Troeltsch's *Social*

Teachings of the Christian Churches—at that time an untranslated study of the diverse relationships that churches and sects assumed to their culture. In that work Troeltsch suggested that differences between churches and sects were derived less from points of doctrine than from more basic sociological factors that set culture-affirming "churches" in opposition to culture denying "sects."

For his first published attempt at scholarly inquiry, Niebuhr set himself to the task of exploring the American religious situation through the church/sect typology Troeltsch constructed for European Christianity. Early in his exploration (and reflecting his own experiences as pastor and president of Elmhurst College), Niebuhr came to the conclusion that religious belief and doctrine were less important to the shape of American Protestantism than social and racial differences. In describing the background to *Social Sources*, Niebuhr confessed that he found the study of belief and doctrine "a procedure so artifical and fruitless that [I] found [myself] compelled to turn from theology to history, sociology, and ethics for a more satisfactory account of denominational differences" (vii). Of these social sciences, history would prove the most important for the clear evidences it provided of a culture-bound American church.

While sharing Troeltsch's conception that religious movements could be fruitfully classified according to their degree of culture-accommodation or culture-alienation, Niebuhr recognized that the American experience required a new type. Virtually all of Troeltsch's culture-accommodating "churches" enjoyed the power and privilege of state support. Conversely, most "sects" were coerced into situations where, even if tolerated, they had to accommodate to the established churches. Such a situation would not prevail in the American republic. The U.S. Constitution and First Amendment meant there could no longer be national churches or religious tests of office. The result was a situation novel to Christianity: a radically voluntarized religious sweepstakes in which religious movements rose or fell solely according to their ability to persuade groups of Americans to follow and support them.

To describe this new religious situation, Niebuhr added a new type labeled "denomination." He employed the term "denominationalism" to describe a religious system comprised of diverse, equally legitimate and purely voluntary religious associations that derived from religious freedom. Denominationalism, in Niebuhr's usage, was both fact and ideology. It not only described a unique situation, but alongside it was the American conviction that this was the way religion *ought* to be practiced. The question then became why Americans voluntarily chose one denomination over against another. Was there an underlying principle that accounted for the unprecedented diversity of religious groups in America?

In answer to this question Niebuhr confirmed Ernest Troeltsch's thesis that social variables determined religious affiliation. The more he studied America's religious past and present, the more certain he became that social factors on the American continent were not consequences of diverse doctrines, but were, rather, the very "sources" of denominationalism. To document such a pattern Niebuhr ranged broadly and freely through the denominational literature of the United States, confirming the high correlations between denominational affiliation and wealth, region, ethnicity and race. Of particular note here were his pioneering explorations of the immigrant church's ambivalent reception/rejection of American culture, and his study of the black church as a movement forged on the crucible of slavery and sustained by the hatreds of white racism. Neither of these groups found acceptance in the Protestant "mainstream," nor did the poor, or the regionally remote.

These shortcomings led Niebuhr to the rueful conclusion that the history of denominationalism in America was not so unlike the Old World "history of schism." Judged according to the universal gospel of the Scriptures, America's novel creation of denominationalism was a failed idea. Although its liberating ethos was important in principle, in fact it seemed only to promote social discrimination and discord. The more successful Niebuhr's social categories were in accounting for the shape of denominationalism in America, the more American Christianity stood under the condemnation of a universal, non-discriminatory gospel.

Secular historians and sociologists were not interested, for the most part, in moving from Niebuhr's correlations of denominations and social variables to his condemnation of denominationalism. But they were driven to further research by the concept of the typology itself, and the question of denominationalism's unique structure and function in the American republic. In general, sociologists concentrated their attention on elaborating types of religiosity, while historians concentrated on the idea of denominationalism.

Literally hundreds of sociological studies have appeared in the past fifty years that specify the Troeltsch/Niebuhr typology, and that update the extent to which modern denominations continue to evidence social sources. In the most recent study of American religion since World War II, Robert Wuthnow discovers a great "restructuring" of the significance and boundaries of denominationalism. But this restructuring continues to confirm Niebuhr's original thesis. Correlations between denominational affiliation and social class, race, and, to a lesser extent, region, persist, even though there is more movement across religious boundaries than that which prevailed in the 1920's (Robert Wuthnow, *The Restructuring of American Religion: Society and Faith Since World War II* [Princeton: Princeton University Press, 1988], 83 – 99).

Historians influenced by *Social Sources* focused their attention less on empirical analyses of social composition than on the phenomenon of denominationalism itself. How does a denominational society come to be, and what is its significance? Major essays by Sidney Mead, Winthrop Hudson, and Timothy Smith moved beyond *Social Sources* by documenting the rise of denominationalism in relation to republican ideology and pluralism. Here it becomes possible to see America's evolving acceptance of voluntarism as both cause and effect of America's more general democratic revolution.

Most recently historians have explored the black church and confirmed in copious, often painful, detail the accuracy of Niebuhr's pioneering observation that "the causes of the racial schism are not difficult to determine. Neither theology nor polity furnished the occasion for it. The sole source of this denominationalism is social; it demonstrates clearly the invasion of the church of Christ by the principle of caste" (*Social Sources*, 259).

While most religious historians writing in post-World War II America evidenced their debt to Niebuhr's categories of analysis in *Social Sources*, they did not always share the gloomy fatalism that pervaded his strictures on denominations. Sidney Mead's essays were particularly important here as corrective to the unallayed bitterness that led Niebuhr to condemn denominations as "ethical failures." In Mead's (and later Timothy Smith's) essays we see that denominations can fulfill positive functions by serving as vital—but safe—competititors in a pluralistic society that values "persuasion" and voluntarism over all attempts at coerced unification.

With the signal exception of race, members of most denominations were not as divided as their combative rhetoric and social cleavages suggest. Through denominationalism, entirely new religious movements proliferated in every generation, keeping the flow of piety steady, even as it moved in ever different channels. In examining nineteenth-century revivals Timothy Smith showed, for example, how denominations could transcend their differences through the mechanism of revivals, and unite in the sort of vast pan-Protestant associations for reform and social transformation that lie behind all periods of political reform in American history. It is this notion of safe competition that explains why denominationalism could be divisive but not cause for violent confrontation, and why there is today a rising incidence of denominational switching across Protestant, Catholic and Jewish boundaries.

Social Sources was not the end of Niebuhr's historical interests, but rather the prelude to a decade of intensive immersion in American religious sources that spanned three centuries of American experience. These investigations would lead to his greatest historical writing, *The Kingdom of God in America*. From the opening pages it is obvious that in the course of writing this book Niebuhr's mind had changed. In now famous words, he repudiated his earlier monocausal emphasis on the social sources of denominationalism, arguing that "though the sociological approach helped to explain why the religious stream flowed in these particular [denominational] channels it did not account for the force of the stream itself" (*Kingdom of God*, vii). When not of limited help, the "sociological approach" was downright diabolical in its tendency to render the religious dimension epiphenomenal, and subordinate it to more "basic" political or economic interests. Some years later, in his Austin Lectures on *Christ and Culture* (1951), Niebuhr conceded that while "it is an aberration of faith as well as of reason to absolutize the finite," nevertheless there is a divine absolute placing all this "relative history of finite men and movements . . . under the governance of the absolute God" (xii).

Niebuhr's increasing concern for the integrity of religion *qua* religion in historical analysis moved him away from concerns with the sociological variables that set denominations apart from one another, and toward a more cultural or anthropological concern with the symbolic commonalities of religious experience—what created unity in the midst of diversity, and testified to the culture-shaping power of religion. This shift in emphasis represented something of a methodological or epistemological conversion in "point of view" that Niebuhr would later term a shift from an "external" observer's interest in structure and function to an "internal" participant's interest in a common "community of memory" premised on shared faith (see *The Meaning of Revelation*).

With an insider's point of view, Niebuhr approached the American religious experience to discover common themes that shaped both Christian and American experience in the New World. Such a search required years of reading. In place of secondary denominational histories, Niebuhr turned to the writings of major religious figures and immersed himself in their worlds. English and American Puritans, Pennsylvania Quakers and Presbyterians, nineteenth century revivalists and Unitarians, Walter Rauschenbusch and, most exhaustively, Jonathan Edwards appear in the pages of *Kingdom of God*, testifying to the astonishing range of his research. Where earlier historians had read deeply in the literature of one denomination or one century, none had dared to grapple with the full sweep of American Protestantism from colonial origins to the twentieth century.

Just as remarkable as the research behind *Kingdom of God* was the thesis it advanced. In all of the variety and shouting competition that set groups of Protestants apart from one another, Niebuhr extracted a common core of meaning and ethos that centered around the impulse to transform the raw American environment into the kingdom of God. Here was something in American Protestantism that Niebuhr could celebrate and endorse even as he condemned the divisiveness of denominations. One cannot read the preface to *Kingdom of God* without picking up the sense of excitement that accompanies all great discoveries. After years of research (and hope) he finally had it: "It appeared possible, then, that the expectation of the kingdom of God on earth was the great common element in our faith and that by reference to it one might be able to understand not only the unity beneath the diversity of American religion but also the effect of Christianity on [American] culture" (*Kingdom of God*, ix). This theme or "dominant idea" (ibid., x), Niebuhr continued, was not some "*a priori* design" (ibid., xi) he imposed on American experience, but rather a pattern that emerged only after repeated sightings in the literature of America's past. Like all great history writings, Niebuhr's immersion in the sources thrust upon him an interpretive framework he had not originally set out to define.

The great contribution of *Kingdom of God* was to establish religion as the central category in American history. Until then, the central categories of interpretation in American historiography were fixed largely without reference to religion. To the extent that it was recognized at all, theology was perceived as a dead language that had to be retranslated into what Vernon Parrington termed the "modern equivalents" of political and economic commentary. The "main themes" of American history were to be found in environmental forces such as the economic interests of the Founding Fathers (Charles Beard) or the frontier (Frederick Jackson Turner). In place of the prevailing assumption that "political and economic interests are alone real," Niebuhr substituted religious faith as the basic factor in American history. In so doing he closed the gap between "American history" and "church history" in ways that made each the product of, as well as the stimulus for, the other.

Any change in main theme necessarily changes the periodization and the main events of American history. Once discovered, organizing principles determine what will be brought into the story and what will be left out. Thus, for example, earlier historians interested in the rise of democratic governments as the main theme in American history filtered their history through a "presidential synthesis" that marked time and significant events according to the rise of new political parties or major presidents. Others, emphasizing economic interest, concentrated on the rise of a commercial class in colonial America and the nineteenth-century Industrial Revolution. And still others, emphasizing environment, looked to the frontier as a great safety valve, and to its closing as the end of an era.

Through his emphasis on faith as the basic factor in American history, Niebuhr would have to engage in a similar filtering of America's past. If faith was to be the main theme not only of churches but of all American history, then all the periodizations and points of emphasis would have to be reoriented and reinterpreted. This Niebuhr managed to do in the remarkably brief span of 200 pages—a feat comparable to Frederick Jackson Turner's brief exposition on the significance of the frontier in American history.

What are the hinge dates of American history when viewed through the filter of faith in a coming kingdom? As Niebuhr traced the kingdom theme through three centuries of American experience, he discovered three distinct emphases that divided history into three distinct periods. In the beginning, American history was dominated by a transplanted Reformation worldview that placed primary emphasis on the "sovereignty of God." The model was monarchical and aristocratic, but balanced by a vision of divine sovereignty so uncompromising that it tended to keep all human institutions (including the church) limited in power.

In the mid-eighteenth century Great Awakening, emphasis shifted from the sovereignty of God to the democratic interest in a more immediate and personal "kingdom of Christ" that gave scope to ever-expanding New World liberties. As the nineteenth century wore on, the emphasis shifted once more in a decisive, transforming way to an orientation around the Social Gospel and the "kingdom on earth."

These three manifestations of one single idea would constitute the dividing markers of American history. All of them incorporated both a religious and a cultural significance. America was a place in which church history was at once national history, for it was a culture whose deepest definitions of self and corporate purpose were embedded in the very language of theology that Parrington hoped to expunge from historical reality.

Like earlier political and economic historians, Niebuhr discovered that great transformations and epoch-making events do not occur without pain and crisis. The transition from one kingdom motif to another was wrenching. It upset the stability that denominations-as-institutions always craved, and called into question all the human authorities that claimed to represent the divine center. Yet such turmoil was necessary, even laudable, for it broke down the old boundaries and allowed religion to grow with the American republic. The kingdom remained the central theme in American history because religious institutions were forever jostled and challenged by the movement of new ideas and creative leaders who pushed faith beyond set categories, and energized a people whose soul travelled along a religious highway.

Of all the transforming movements that shaped American society, the one Niebuhr singled out for special attention and emphasis—because it was the first—was the Great Awakening. In this event, inherited religious ideas and emerging New World realities came together in a new and potent configuration that would prefigure, and pave the way for, the subsequent American Revolution. The revivals of religion inspired by Jonathan Edwards and George Whitefield were *the* shaping events of early America. They represented, in Niebuhr's words, "an awakening to God that was simultaneous with its awakening to national self-consciousness. It was no wholly new beginning, for the Christianity expressed in it was a more venerable thing than the American nation. Yet for America it was a new beginning; it was our national conversion" (*Kingdom of God*, 126). Through the mechanism of mass revivals, the Christ-centered, tolerant spirituality of the seventeenth century Quakers came to be appropriated in Protestant churches generally, creating a new, voluntaristic configuration of Christians and their democratic culture in which "an order of liberty and love had been substituted for the order of regimentation and fear" (ibid., 90). In this sense, the Great Awakening marked the real American Revolution.

As Niebuhr's new point of view radically revised the main themes of American history, it also challenged much of the existing church history written from denominational perspectives. Many church historians, embarrassed by the extremes of popular piety manifested in the revivals, wrote them off to a misguided zeal that temporarily overran its denominational banks. Others recognized their significance, but marked it primarily in rising church membership rates and the creation of new evangelical denominations.

For Niebuhr, on the other hand, the primary significance of the Great Awakening was to be found in the generation— or rather regeneration—of a pan-Protestant, culture-transforming movement that upset denominations far more than it founded them. A handful of new denominations on top of an already large number would not transform a nation. But inclusive revivals, interdenominational missions, schools, textbooks, social reforms, and a spirit of disestablishment would. Underlying the transforming radicalism of the Great Awakening was a new-found humility derived from the power of "reconciliation to Being, to the divine reality," (*Kingdom of God*, 103) that stood above and apart from all human institutions, creeds and systems of faith. Through this powerful reconciliation came a renewed vision of community and kingdom that registered the new trust Americans would invest in themselves and their covenant God.

All revolutions require founding parents and, in Niebuhr's case, the founder of record was not George Washington, or Thomas Jefferson, or Abraham Lincoln, but Jonathan Edwards. Though Edwards was never politically active and died before the Revolution, Niebuhr saw in him an "American Augustine" (*Kingdom of God*, xiv) who so embodied the spirit of the new revivals that his life and mind could not be separated from the event he struggled so mightily to defend. At the very moment when the "paralysis of institutionalization" (*Kingdom of God*, 165) seemed ready to strangle the churches, Edwards breathed into the old forms a new spirit that fit with the dawning birth of a new nation.

The moving force in Edwards' revival was not his intellect or his democratic sensibilities so much as his unblinking view of a sovereign God whose very being challenged all other denominational, cultural or political pretensions to divinity. Whenever a religious community is serious about the reality of divine sovereignty, there is automatically a crisis of faith in all else.

More than any of his peers Edwards grasped, or experienced, the crisis of human frailty caught in the hands of an angry but loving God. As such, Niebuhr concluded, Edwards was not the anachronistic "wreck on the remote sands of time" that earlier critics contended (Stuart Pratt Sherman, *Life and Letters of Stuart Pratt Sherman*, ed. Jacob Zeitlin and Homer Woodbridge, 2 vols. [New York: Farrar & Rinehart, 1929] 1: 263), so much as he was a voice of modernity whose blasts at religious pride issued from an "intense awareness of the precariousness of life's poise, of the utter insecurity of men and of mankind which are at every moment as ready to plunge into the abyss of disintegration, barbarism, crime and the war of all against all, as to advance toward harmony and integration. He recognized what Kierkegaard meant when he described life as treading water with ten thousand fathoms beneath us" (*Kingdom of God*, 137–38).

Alongside revivalism, Niebuhr introduced millennialism as a central factor in *Kingdom of God*. The eschatological implications of the kingdom motif were not lost on Niebuhr, and he explored them thoroughly in his chapter on "The Coming Kingdom." To be sure, other scholars had noted Americans' penchant for millennial rhetoric, but none had demonstrated the systematic connections of millennialism to revivalism and social reform. Niebuhr recognized that while Americans hardly invented millennialism, they gave it modern expression by identifying it with the American republic. Millennial speculations did not cease with awakening and independence, but actually gained in force and credibility throughout the nineteenth century.

The significance of millennial themes could be registered in the Second Great Awakening, in the emergence of new adventist religious movements, and most importantly, in the impulse toward social reform. Through the language and imagery of millennialism, social reformers moved forward, confident in their campaigns to restructure American society, and confident that "a Christian revolution was evidently taking place; a new day was dawning" (ibid., 148).

It would be difficult to overstate the impact *Kingdom of God* had in revising American historians' understanding of their nation and the forces that helped shape it. In his seminal essay on "The Recovery of American Religious History," Henry F. May credited *Kingdom of God* with informing "many of the ablest religious historians of the next period" (*American Historical Review* 70 [1964] 85). Chief among these historians was Perry Miller, an admirer of H. Richard Niebuhr. His magisterial studies of *Jonathan Edwards* (1949) and *The New England Mind: From Colony to Province* (1953) were in many respects a massive elaboration of the periodization and conceptualizations set forth in *Kingdom of God*.

In tracing the critical moments of transformation that marked America's movement from colony to nation, Miller identified the Great Awakening as *the* watershed in America's cultural and intellectual evolution. The Great Awakening, Miller later asserted, was not simply a dramatic event but a "veritable crisis in the indigenous civilization" (*Errand into the Wilderness* [Cambridge: Harvard University Press, 1956], 157). Elsewhere he described it as "a transformaton, a blaze that consumed the theological universe of the seventeenth century, and left the American wilderness to rake the embers for a new concept of meaning" (*Errand*, 154). In discovering new meanings the revivalists spoke in democratic, religious and theological terms of a new order that anticipated the redefinition of "the relation of the ruler—political or ecclesiastical—to the body politic" (ibid., 156).

Just as Jonathan Edwards served as *figura* for the Great Awakening in *Kingdom of God*, so also did he provide a dramatic center to

Miller's narrative. Far from being a retrograde theologian, Miller concluded, Edwards was so far ahead of his time "that our own can hardly be said to have caught up with him" (*Jonathan Edwards* [New York: W. Sloane Associates, 1949], xxxii). Edwards confronted the crisis of his age, and pointed the way to a new movement even as "his own Yale disowned him" (*Jonathan Edwards*, 197). That new movement was inescabably democratic and egalitarian. Through his writings on revival, Edwards was "telling what in political terms the revival really meant: that the leader has the job of accommodating himself to the realities of human and, in any particular situation, of social, experience. No matter what he may have as an assured creed, as a dogma—no matter what he may be able to pronounce, in the terms of abstract theology, concerning predestination and original sin—as a public leader he must adapt himself to public welfare and calamity" (*Errand*, 164). In these and countless other places one can sense the background voice of Niebuhr, and his insistence that the revival was the characteristic expression of the American people's search for national identity. One can believe in the covenant as Niebuhr did, or disbelieve it as Miller did, but in either case its centrality to the American errand is unmistakable.

Since Perry Miller, historians have continued to explore the role of revivalism in American history. Major interpretive works by Alan Heimert and William G. McLoughlin have made it impossible to ignore the role revivalism has played in shaping a national identity. In a recent essay, McLoughlin argues convincingly that the Great Awakening represents the key to understanding the American Revolution: "The roots of the Revolution as a political movement were so deeply imbedded in the soil of the First Great Awakening forty years earlier that it can be truly said that the Revolution was the natural outgrowth of that profound and widespread religious movement" (William G. McLoughlin, " 'Enthusiasm for Liberty': The Great Awakening as the Key to the Revolution," *Proceedings of the American Antiquarian Society* 87 [1977] 70). In like manner Heimert organized his massive study of *Religion and the American Mind*(1966) around the now famous thesis that "evangelical religion, which had as its most notable formal expression the 'Calvinism' of Jonathan Edwards, was not the retrograde philosophy that many historians rejoice to see confounded in America's

Age of Reason. Rather, Calvinism, and Edwards, provided pre-Revolutionary America with a radical, even democratic, social and political ideology, and evangelical religion embodied, and inspired, a thrust toward American nationalism" (Alan Heimert, *Religion and the American Mind*, [Cambridge: Harvard University Press, 1966] viii).

If any religious subject has exceeded revivalism in interest and creative breakthroughs, that subject would be millennialism. Indeed, it could plausibly be argued that explorations of American millennialism constitute *the* interpretive theme of the 1970s and '80s. Sacvan Bercovitch's pioneering exploration of millennial themes in the Puritan jeremiad, C. C. Goen's treatment of Edwards' post-millenialism, Albert Raboteau's analysis of the "black jeremiad," Nathan Hatch's discussion of the eschatological meaning of American wars with France, Ruth Bloch's study of a "visionary republic," James Moorhead's description of the Civil War as an "American Apocalypse," Bruce Kuklick's study of American philosophy, and William R. Hutchison's development of "the liberal emphasis upon an earthly kingdom of God" all confirm Niebuhr's early intuition that:

> [t]he rise in American faith of the idea of the coming kingdom was not due to an importation from the outside, that is, from rationalism or political idealism. It arose out of the Christian movement which had begun with the conviction of divine sovereignty, been led thence to the realization of Christ's kingdom and now saw clearly that the latter led toward the realization of man's everlasting hope (*Kingdom of God*, 143).

If much recent history writing has confirmed H. Richard Niebuhr's instincts about the religious factor in American history, it has also furnished materials for constructive critique. Running throughout Niebuhr's writings is an anti-institutional bias that sets up an ongoing dialectic between "order" and "movement," where order signifies stagnation and ossification, and movement, dynamism and prophetic godliness. The kingdom motif that Niebuhr found running throughout American history was not only comprehensive and engaging but remarkably adaptive, a protean shape whose outline could never be fixed. Indeed, it was this adaptive quality that led Niebuhr to identify kingdom language with ongoing movements powerful enough to counter the impulse toward stasis, complacency, and self-satisfaction. Niebuhr could both condemn denominations and endorse the kingdom motif in American history, because in celebrating the kingdom he did not have to identify it with any single (and therefore "superior") denomination. The referent to the kingdom symbol lay outside and beyond denominational history. Thus Niebuhr could separate out that which was transformative or transcendent in all denominations from that which retarded movement or placed its hope in human institutions.

It was precisely the order/movement dialectic that led H. Richard Niebuhr to perceive revivals and awakenings as positive dimensions of faith, while intervening periods of institutional calm were times of stagnation and mere moralism. Yet recent scholarship provides evidence that qualifies both the affirmations and condemnations of these polar extremes.

In looking first at the revivals as indices of spiritual movement, it is important to see how much they reflected social sources that are as discernable and measurable as the sorts of social patterns Niebuhr found undergirding American denominations. If the revivals represented movement, these recent studies suggest, it was a predictable movement: the movement of a young, "temporarily frustrated" and geographically displaced fourth generation. In 1740, the twenty-four-year-old George Whitefield met his most dramatic successes among similarly young admirers. In like manner, the thirty-year-old Jonathan Edwards noted how his Northampton revival began with the young people in the community. The social sources of revivalism have been so thoroughly documented that in a recent article, Jon Butler has been led to question the whole concept of a Great Awakening (Jon Butler, "Enthusiasm Described and Decried: The Great Awakening as Historical Fiction," *Journal of American History* 69 [1982] 305–25).

If celebrations of revivalism need to be curbed by a more sober examination of their social correlates, so, too, periods of institutional calm require a more balanced understanding. There is no better example here than the case of Niebuhr's arch-nemesis Cotton Mather. With the possible exception of twentieth-century Protestant liberals, no one came in for harsher censure in the the work of Niebuhr (and Perry Miller) than Cotton Mather. In unusually strong language, Niebuhr portrayed Mather as one caught in a "febrile subjectivism" that sought to preserve an outmoded, "perverted form":

> With all his eagerly displayed learning he defended the established order ... The law written upon the inward parts was for Cotton Mather an inscription to be endlessly studied in a state of hypochondriac introspection. His *Essays To Do Good* are classic example of inverted moralism. Here all attention is directed toward the self and its moral culture (*Kingdom of God*,171).

Such a one-sided view of Mather is guilty of the same sort of stereotyping Niebuhr lamented in nineteenth-century assessments of Jonathan Edwards. Recent biographies of Mather by Robert Middlekauff, David Levin, and Kenneth Silverman all point to a very different person than the one Niebuhr and Miller loved to hate. Unlike his famous first and second generation ancestors who were notorious for their intolerance and inflexibility, Cotton Mather struck out boldly and relentlessly for a "Christian union" bound in ever-widening webs of Anglo-American association.

Mather remained a strict Congregationalist to his dying day, but this was not the platform from which he trumpeted New England's glory. Rather, New England's virtue was measured, as in other Protestant churches and nations, by its willingness to forge an "evangelical" union of "piety and morality" that would confront the powers of darkness, and speed the course of God's coming millennial kingdom. To be part of this united front, people did not have to be Congregationalists as his forefathers insisted, but they did have to be zealous for "well-doing": "Let no man pretend unto the name of a Christian, who does not approve the proposal of a perpetual endeavor to do good in the world" (Cotton Mather, *Bonifacius: An Essay Upon the Good*, ed. David Levin [Cambridge: Harvard University Press, 1966], 18–19). By prescribing a realm of ecumenical cooperation in voluntary "reforming societies," Mather hoped to free the New England churches to move in ever broader associations toward precisely the sort of Christian union that Niebuhr identified with the "Protestant Movement."

If re-examinations of revivalism and Cotton Mather do not in any way diminish H. Richard Niebuhr's achievement, they do point out the dangers of one-sided historical emphases, and the limitations of a dialectical method that goes on to arrange its polarities in ethical categories of "good" and "bad." In Niebuhr's case, the lopsided praise of movement to the virtual exclusion of order can yield the mistaken image of (to paraphrase him) a church without creeds bringing people without codes into a kingdom without structure through the ministrations of crises without end. Such a view is as problematic as works of denominational triumphalism that ascribe all to the institution of "their" denomination and its creedal "Truth."

Interestingly enough, Niebuhr,in his later essay on *The Meaning of Revelation* (1941), put forward a concept of the church that implied an institutionalization of sorts, structured around a core "community of memory" derived from the person of Jesus Christ and the Christian scriptures. This instituted church, he observed, is wider in orientation than any particular denomination or nation, but it does seek an order alongside movement that is rooted in transcendence:

> The standpoint of the Christian community is limited, being in history, faith and sin. But what is seen from this standpoint is unlimited ... But as reason, having learned through limited experience an intelligible pattern of reality, can seek the evidence of a like pattern in all other experience, so faith having apprehended the divine self in its own history, can and must look for the manifestation of the same self in all other events (*Meaning of Revelation*, 86–87).

It is regrettable that Niebuhr never brought the separate insights of *Social Sources*, *Kingdom of God*, and *Meaning of Revelation* together in one synthetic study that would have completed his model of faith as the basic factor in American history. Such a model would simultaneously recognize the social sources of all religious activity and try to find in the rich diversity the workings of one divine mind and will. Perhaps the closest equivalent we have to such a broad-based study is Sydney Ahlstrom's monumental survey of religious experience, *A Religious History of the American People* (1972).

Criticisms of Niebuhr's writings are bound to continue, but they are themselves tributes to the power of his historical imagination. Like all great historians, Niebuhr had a gift that cannot be taught or readily imitated. That gift was the ability to intuit in advance of empirical, monographic research a model of the organizing patterns and symbolic polarities of past experience. Through Niebuhr's powerful intuition, past and present came together in ways that not only heighten our appreciation of faith as the main theme in America's past, but also press upon us the responsbility for discerning moral lessons to apply to the present. In so doing we are challenged to take our place in a community of memory, cherishing a kingdom that ultimately knows no national boundaries, and whose destination has been marked from eternity. Such was the kingdom of H. Richard Niebuhr.

6

Response to Harry Stout

William R. Hutchison

Harry Stout's paper reminds us not only of H. Richard Niebuhr's accomplishments as a historian, and of the specific lines of inquiry he induced us to pursue, but also of Niebuhr's importance in presenting comprehensive groundplans for American religious historiography. Stout attributes much of the unusual inspirational force in these broad proposals (ground plans often are dull, easily filed away) to Niebuhr's theological convictions, together with his willingness to make those convictions explicit, his readiness even to risk being wrong or hyperbolic, and to have to correct himself.

As Quakers would put it, "way was open" for someone to present such seminal, originating constructs. Niebuhr's writings on American history are works of real genius, and would have been such in any era. Yet the condition of such subfields as religious and theological history did affect or even determine the nature of his contributions.

The condition I refer to, of course, is the primitive state of these subfields in the decades when Niebuhr was writing. "That was then, this is now," and the contrast between then and now—as reflected, for example, in the recently published *Encyclopedia of the American Religious Experience*—is quite astounding. Before the

1950s, so little was going on in American religious history, so few laborers were working that vineyard, that Niebuhr *had* to answer and perhaps contradict himself, to play both offense and defense. Had the historical game been football, we could scarcely have fielded two teams, let alone two platoons per team.

But wasn't this situation much improved, by the 1950s, at places like Yale and Harvard? Not really. A little personal vantage may be helpful.

As a doctoral student in history at Yale in 1953, when I trudged up the hill to seek mentors at the Divinity School, I experienced several minor shocks or setbacks. The first shock was Roland Bainton, who astounded me not so much by his erudition, great as that was, but by his capacity for learning names and faces. On the first day of classes I tried Bainton's large course on the social teachings of the Christian churches. Finding that this course was not the one I needed at the moment, I enrolled instead in Bob Michaelsen's seminar in American religious history. A month or so later, I finally met Bainton at a social event. "I'm Bill Hutchison," I announced. "I know," he said. "What happened?"

The next trauma came when Michaelsen was shot out from under me, so to speak. Bob had left the University of Iowa just a couple of years earlier. Now, to punish him for leaving in the first place, Iowa was making him dean, and off he went. So I felt stranded. I went to Michaelsen and asked what would become of me. Bob thought about it, then suggested I importune H. Richard Niebuhr for some tutorials in American religious history. "He will say that he's not really a historian; that he did write books in the field, but long ago; and that he hasn't kept in touch. But then he will do it."

I accepted Michaelsen's advice, partly because I figured that one extra hour a week would make little difference in a professor's schedule. (I no longer figure that.) I visited Niebuhr in his small office, where the desk faced the wall in order that professor and visitor could face each other directly. After I had made my proposal, there was a very long pause, during which Niebuhr stared straight at the wall. Then he said, "I'm not really a historian. I did write those books, but that was a long time ago, and I haven't kept up. But I guess we can do it."

We did do it, greatly to my advantage. Niebuhr was scarcely out of touch with the historiography of American religion; it would not be a great exaggeration to say—paraphrasing Perry Miller's remark about Jonathan Edwards—that he could have read some Sidney Mead and Winthrop Hudson and been caught up completely. Besides, he had just produced *Christ and Culture,* and was especially primed to help with the kind of comparative work I was determined to pursue. He suggested the investigations of Coleridge's American influence that led to my doctoral thesis. And as I'll have occasion to comment, the impress of Niebuhr's then current preoccupations was to become even more important to me later.

The point at the moment, however, is that the field of American religious history was almost bare. There were few to whom one could turn, at Yale or anywhere, for originating structures, or even for a genuine determination to take seriously both religion and history. The field was fortunate indeed that Niebuhr chose in his writings to respond to the resulting demand (which, as Stout says, resonated with demands of his own nature).

My first direct comment on the points in Harry Stout's paper is a suggested addition. I suspect that *Christ and Culture,* even though not "American history," may have had as much influence upon the development of our field as either of the earlier books Stout discusses. Just how many other scholars in American religious history were influenced by the *Christ and Culture* stage of Niebuhr's thinking I don't know; it would be hard to say, since such influences, however powerful, become diffused as they combine with various others. But I, at least, have had the experience of working thirty years later in a more fundamental way with those categories than I did at the outset.

One of my observations, in introducing a recent book on missionary thought, was that the problem of the missionary "was the problem of Christ and culture squared." That was not just a cute remark, or at least it was not intended as such. I meant that as I had struggled to understand and sort out cross-cultural problems of religious transmission, Niebuhr's categories had come to my aid. My impression is that, for scholars in the American field, that happens even more often with the "Christ and culture" problematic than with Niebuhr's insights concerning the kingdom motif—if only because the former, in this context at least, is more nearly a unique contribution.

Certainly Stout is right, however, about the overwhelming importance of both *The Social Sources of Denominationalism* and *The Kingdom of God in America*. *Social Sources* provided a needed corrective—not for most of the secular historians, who needed no persuading about the shaping force of social-economic circumstance, but more for the Church and denominational historians, who by and large had continued to believe that denominatinal marriages and sectarian divorces were made in heaven. (Some still do believe that, which is one reason seminary courses still use Niebuhr's book.)

Stout is also right that *Kingdom of God* has been tremendously influential as well as respected. This is true, as I think Stout is saying, in at least three ways. The book was important for its reassertion that religion shapes history as well as is shaped by it. Second, it ranks as one of the great founding interpretations of what we might call "redeemer nation" scholarship among cultural, literary, religious, and comparative historians. (Stylistically, it ranks as one of the very best in that genre.) Third, *Kingdom of God* provided sub-categories—the sovereignty of God, the kingdom of Christ, the coming kingdom—that one may want to rearrange sequentially or disturb in other ways, but that one *can* rearrange and keep using precisely because Niebuhr, with characteristic finesse and humility, kept them from seeming procrustean.

Before moving on from Niebuhr's *Kingdom of God*, I'll put a second, direct question or suggestion to Stout. I wonder if he goes too far, farther than Niebuhr himself wished to go, when he speaks of the kingdom interpretation as *displacing* other fundamental interpretations of American history. I don't read Niebuhr as claiming that much. In at least one important passage Niebuhr did seem to propose that the kingdom idea—even in its biblical, unsecularized form—was the key to American history. But for the most part he spoke more modestly of the reinterpretation of American *religion*, and of the kingdom idea as the "distinctive note in American Christianity."

I don't think Stout and I are far apart here. Yet the distinction I'm making isn't just a quibble. The degree to which Niebuhr, in insisting upon the force and autonomy of religious motives, intended to jettison economic and other interpretations, is a fairly important matter to consider in judging his contributions and influence.

But I agree, in general and in most detail, with Stout's estimate of the importance to American religious history of the two books that were explicitly in that area. By making the differently structured *Christ and Culture* equally seminal for American studies, I may be generalizing too readily from my own experience. Despite that, let me make another suggestion in passing that could be biased in the same way.

It seems to me that Niebuhr, especially through the modalities represented in *Christ and Culture*, contributed almost as much to the recovery and restudy of the *liberal* traditions as to our understanding of revivalism, or millennialism, or the morphology of religious institutions. This is too much to elaborate upon here, but I should clarify: I am referring to Niebuhr's reappropriations of Bushnell, Emerson, and others in the liberal theological tradition, and not just to his interest in the social gospel. Along with Shelton Smith and some others of the high neo-orthodox generation, Niebuhr participated in what the preacher George A. Gordon would have called a "deeper return" to the sources and most vital expressions of liberalism. But of course "return" may not be quite appropriate in Niebuhr's case. The author of the famous "God without wrath" quote, despite that scathing summation, had never proposed wholesale jettisoning of the liberal/modernist heritage.

To recall that Niebuhr could be engaged as much with Bushnell as with Edwards is also to realize that his writings conveyed the excitement of inner dialogues along with the stimulation of overall visions. The initial success and usefulness of his interpretations might be explained by the rudimentary condition of scholarship and conceptualization in religious history. Their staying power, the fact that we still use and assign his books, of course, cannot be explained that way.

In 1960, the late Clifton Olmstead produced a comprehensive history of American religion that was noteworthy for being the first such treatment since William Warren Sweet's, and for reflecting a greater inclusiveness than either Sweet or Niebuhr had achieved in their generation. Yet Robert S. Michaelsen, in reviewing Olmstead's book, felt obliged to warn readers about a certain tediousness. He opened his review by recalling the famous Thurber cartoon in which an exasperated man asks a recumbent, pouting woman, "Well, who *made* the magic go out of our marriage, you or me?"

Where there is too little vision, the people may not perish. We shall in any case need to rely, from time to time, on the more tedious textbooks. But we prefer vision, or even a little magic. Teachers as well as students will continue to gravitate toward works that embody those qualities.

Even more surely, historians of American religion will continue to honor and gain inspiration from this theologian, H. Richard Niebuhr, who was one of the founders and shapers of their discipline.

7

H. Richard Niebuhr
and the Task of a Public Theology

Linell E. Cady

Several years ago, when I was doing some work on Josiah Royce, I hit upon the idea of "public theology" as a way to articulate the commendable features in his thought that I considered useful guideposts for contemporary theology. Although I found a few scattered references to the term, it certainly was not a designation that had any wide currency. In the last year or so, however, I have seen a flurry of references to public theology and public religion. This explosion of interest, I have come to see in retrospect, was not really all that sudden. Its roots were there, albeit often hidden behind other formulations and scattered amongst a variety of issues having to do with religion and public life.

Multiple topics and perspectives are reflected in this emerging interest in religion and public life. Perhaps the central theme in this medley of concerns is a growing critique, from all ends of the ideological spectrum, of the privatization of religion. Dissatisfaction with the purported displacement of religious beliefs and values from the public realm has precipitated significant discussion over their appropriate role in the determination of public policy, and has sparked renewed interest in the phenomenon of civil religion. It has also spawned numerous historical and theoretical studies on issues of church-state relations in American life. Another facet of this growing interest in religion and public life is the collective effort by a number of theologians to counteract their academic marginalization by striving to identify and engage in public discourse and argumentation.

The diversity of issues potentially connected with the notion of public theology threatens to overwhelm the concept, rendering it so fluid, so indefinite, that it leads to more obscurity than clarity. On the other hand, the protean nature of the concept is also the source of its strength. Its value, it seems to me, lies precisely in its ability to bring together and address a number of these disparate but related issues.

The integrative power of the notion of public theology can be glimpsed by considering the meaning of the term "public" over against several of its contraries. The meaning of public takes on different nuances depending upon that to which it is being contrasted. It can, for instance, be understood in opposition to parochial. In this context public suggests that which is open to all or intelligible to all, while parochial denotes some circumscription in availability or intelligibility. In common parlance the circumscription is typically attributed to a religious affiliation that is not universally shared.

Public can also, however, be contrasted with private. This opposition suggests the difference between the individual and society, between the personal or intimate realm of life and the wider social and political realm. Finally, public can be contrasted with professional. Here, again, public suggests the whole without discrimination, while professional circumscribes a subset of the whole based not upon religious affiliation but upon occupational training and affiliation.

My aim in this paper is to develop a model for a public theology, considering in the process the three senses of public noted above. My procedure will not be simply to affirm the meaning of public that contrasts with the parochial, the private, and the professional. Rather, by working with these polarities I shall attempt to develop a revised interpretation of public, one that builds upon the strengths of, but avoids the ahistorical and individualistic biases that infect our current understanding of public. This procedure will enable me to clarify the methodological characteristics of public theology, to indicate the substantive agenda in this form of theological reflection, and to consider questions of style and audience that are appropriate to public discourse. I will carry out my discussion of public theology with reference to H. Richard Niebuhr, whose work, in many respects, has struck me as an example of this form of theology.

I should say that my fastening upon Niebuhr as an example was more the result of an intuitive flash than an extensive canvassing of the field in light of my model. I say this not to confer credibility on the choice, but to acknowledge the possibility of other appropriate examples. I am sure that Niebuhr came to mind in part because he has long been one of those thinkers with whom and through whom I have struggled to think theologically. Although I am hardly an expert on his corpus, he is one of a limited number of thinkers with whom I feel connected as a result of greater exposure and appreciation. This is no doubt the case because of the opportunity I have had to study with so many who were deeply influenced by him.

Thinking about public theology in relationship to Niebuhr's work has proven to be both an interesting and productive process. On the one hand, it has cast Niebuhr in a substantially different light for me, helping me to see finally how the author of *Radical Monotheism and Western Culture* could also be the author of *The Meaning of Revelation*. On the other hand, it has helped me to develop more fully, and I think more deeply, the substantive agenda of a public theology. Before pursuing Niebuhr's work as an exemplification of public theology, however, I would like to pause, even if briefly, over the meaning of "public" in an effort to gain some historical perspective on our own sense of the term.

II

It is easy to assume that the contours of our public and private worlds are permanent features of the social landscape. The private world encompasses the individual and family, and perhaps intimate friends. The public realm includes that world beyond our private enclave. These simple definitions do not capture, however, the varying ways in which these spheres can be fashioned and valued.

Recently the ancient Greek vision of public life has elicited considerable attention, largely as a device to gain critical distance from our own social terrain.[1] Attraction to the Greek model has centered upon the egalitarian and dialogic character of Greek public life.[2] Insofar as the *polis* consisted of a community of peers, violence and force were inappropriate. Debate and persuasion, tactics appealing to the heart and mind of the community, were mandated. The ancient Greeks esteemed the public sphere much more highly than the private, regarding it as the domain of freedom wherein human identity and excellence were achieved. Private life, although necessary, carried with it a sense of privation; "it meant literally a state of being deprived of something, and even of the highest and most human of man's capacities."[3] Interest in, if not romanticization of, ancient Greek civic life reflects a growing discontent with the modern construal of public life which bears little resemblance to its Greek counterpart.

Although providing a potentially subversive critical distance from our own interpretation and valuation of public and private life, the Greek alternative does not help us to understand the forces that have contributed to shaping the modern geography of the public and private realms. This is, of course, an enormously complex story that cannot be fully unravelled here. To understand our own interpretations of these spheres, however, we must consider, if only briefly, the effect the Enlightenment has had upon shaping the modern outlook. Long after its official closure, this chapter of our history has continued to exert its effects.

The Enlightenment contribution to the structuring of our public and private spaces was forged in response to a social crisis rooted both in the Protestant Reformation and in the lengthy religious wars that ensued in the sixteenth and seventeenth centuries. Against this backdrop of civil and religious discord, Enlightenment thinkers sought to develop a form of discourse and a minimalist vision of the good that could be shared irrespective of religious affiliation. To reestablish social peace, religion was increasingly

---

[1] See e.g. Hannah Arendt, *The Human Condition* (Chicago: The University of Chicago Press, 1958), 22–78; Jean Bethke Elshtain, *Public Man, Private Woman: Women in Social and Political Thought* (Princeton: Princeton University Press, 1981), 19–54.

[2] It is important to note that this equality was a decidedly restricted affair. It was an equality amongst male citizens, and did not extend to the majority of the population, including slaves, women, and children.

[3] Arendt, *The Human Condition*, 38.

relegated to the private sphere, and a secular discourse was developed to articulate the nature of political and social life. Although this secular discourse, which has come to be called philosophic liberalism, was neither an ahistorical nor an interest-free portrait of human life, it has become so embedded in the personal and political fabric of Western life that it has come to assume a self-evident quality.

Basic to philosophic liberalism is the assumption that human beings are radically autonomous creatures driven by their desires to pursue their own self-interest.[4] Recognizing the dangers of unrestrained egoism, individuals rationally choose to enter into a social contract that will facilitate their personal security and private gain. Society, according to this view, is not based upon any substantive agreement about the good life, nor does it need to be. The optimal society is one that maximizes, as far as possible, the freedom of individuals to secure their private ends.

This radical emphasis upon the freedom and autonomy of the self runs throughout the political, social, and economic theories of classical liberalism. Not only was it eminently suited to the emerging capitalistic economy, which needed to break down traditional social bonds, but it was also a powerful tool in the fight to liberate the social order from the domination of entrenched political and ecclesiastical authorities.

A similar emancipatory thrust lies behind the interpretation of reason developed by Enlightenment thinkers. The unifying thread running through both the rationalist and the empiricist variations was the struggle to escape the control of heteronomous authorities. As Kant argued in his seminal essay, "What Is Enlightenment?", reason consists in the capacity to think for oneself, in the refusal to allow outside authorities to determine sound judgment. The desired independence from authority and tradition was secured by attributing to reason a universal character that was shared by all, irrespective of time and place. Construing reason as an ahistorical capacity that transcends parochial limitations ensured that human inquiry need not depend upon local authorities or traditions for its assumptions and warrants.

---

[4] William M. Sullivan offers a very illuminating account of the nature and development of philosophic liberalism in his work, *Reconstructing Public Philosophy* (Berkeley: University of California Press, 1982).

It is clear that the style of inquiry emerging in the natural sciences in the seventeenth century contributed to the ahistorical, universal character of the Enlightenment model of rationality. Stress was placed upon objectivity, neutrality, and a quantitative approach to knowledge. Insofar as knowledge came to be construed as knowing the facts, it increasingly relegated ideals and goals to non-cognitive status.[5] This trajectory merely reinforced the assumption that ends were a product of individual passions, outside the province of reasoned, public inquiry.

The effects of liberal interpretations of human nature, society, and reason on our public and private topography in recent centuries have been considerable. To achieve its emancipatory and irenic aims, liberalism construes "public" in very expansive and very reductive terms. On the one hand, public is highly inclusive insofar as it encompasses all persons. On the other hand, it does not include those aspects of individuals that make them distinct. It reduces the individual to a least common denominator of personhood, separating the self from the characteristics and roles which determine personal identity. The specifics of individual personal history are irrelevant within the public realm.

This duality in the meaning of public is also reflected in the Enlightenment model of reason. Reason, in its expansive sense, is a universal capacity potentially shared by all human beings. However, it necessarily excludes the historical determinants or prejudices in human reflection that destroy this common character, thereby reducing reason to its technical, instrumental function.[6] Hence public has come to have a very inclusive, but very abstract or formal application.

Enlightenment interpretations of self, society, and reason, and the vision of the public that they generated, were effective tools in the building of modern society. Not only were they well-adapted

---

[5] This was not the position of all Enlightenment theorists, as Kant's writings make clear. Although Kant did not consider moral judgments a form of knowledge, they were a function of the practical employment of reason, and hence not irrational or subjective. Nevertheless, the effects of his distinction between pure and practical reason contributed significantly to the gradual relegation of religion, morality, and aesthetics to a non-cognitive status.

[6] For an illuminating analysis of the Enlightenment's "prejudice against prejudice," see Hans-Georg Gadamer, *Truth and Method* (New York: Seabury Press, 1975), 245–53.

to an increasingly industrialized and capitalized economy, but they also provided the framework and impetus for the embrace of democracy and individual rights, including the right of religious freedom. Without belittling the extraordinary gains achieved by the Enlightenment, we must confront the underside of this vision. Although it continues to dominate the popular ethos, voices of discontent have been growing. Much contemporary philosophy, for instance, has engaged in a sustained critique of the model of rationality that informed the Enlightenment, insisting that reason is inextricably rooted in a specific historical and cultural matrix. Others have targeted the individualistic bias of this vision as an excessive exaggeration which has contributed to a dangerous erosion of communal identity and loyalty. These critiques will become important as I attempt to develop my understanding of public theology. Although they should not blind us to the continuing virtues in the Enlightenment construal of "public," they point the way toward its revision. Such a revision, I shall argue, constitutes both the ground and the goal of a public theology.

III

Public theology can not be interpreted solely in terms of the influences of religion in the public sphere. Theology is a reflective practice which involves the critical reflection upon and transformation of religion. It is necessary, therefore, to consider *how* theology achieves its effects. A public theology not only will address itself to the public realm, but it will do so in a genuinely public fashion. It is this latter stipulation that appears to pose an insurmountable obstacle to the quest for a public theology. For in what possible sense can theology be understood as a form of public discourse and argumentation?

For most people, I suspect, theology represents the quintessential example of parochial inquiry. Rather than appealing to a common human experience, theology roots itself in the experiences and texts of a specific religious community. Instead of employing a discourse that all share, theology appropriates the symbols and motifs of a particular tradition. Rather than engaging in open inquiry, theology appears to take as axiomatic certain "truths" as the givens of its reflection. Theology is parochial in the sense that it addresses a particular religious community, and appeals to the symbols, experiences and texts of that community for its justification. From this perspective, theology is more aptly construed as a product of faith, not reason, as an apologetic exercise that does not embody genuine argumentation at all.

If this depiction of the parochial nature of theology were fully adequate, then we would have no choice but to abandon the quest for a public form of theological inquiry. The depiction, however, conflates two different ways of understanding the parochial nature of theology. The first sense of parochial, perhaps better called contextualism, refers to theology's appropriation of and engagement with the texts, symbols, and experiences of a particular tradition. The second sense dwells upon theology's traditional dependence upon certain first principles or authorities that circumscribe theological argumentation. We must differentiate between the contextual and the dogmatic senses of parochial, because they constitute markedly different obstacles for developing a public theology.

To assume that theology is not a form of public inquiry because of its engagement with a particular tradition presumes a highly misleading, ahistorical sense of public. Rather than acquiesce to this ahistorical notion of public, theologians should help to combat the prejudice against tradition that it reflects. It falsely presumes that reason operates outside of local contexts, that it can escape from the influences of particular traditions of interpretation. It reflects, as we have seen, the Enlightenment legacy that continues to inform our outlook. Developing a public theology, therefore, requires us to revise the Enlightenment construal of public rationality.

It does not, however, require us to abandon completely the Enlightenment model. Although guilty of certain excesses and distortions in its attack upon the obstacles to the genuine exercise of reason, the Enlightment distinction between engaging in open inquiry and citing heteronomous authorities must be retained. If theology aspires to be a form of public reflection, it must abandon the dogmatic warrants and premises of its traditional mode of argumentation.

Although expressed in different terminology, Niebuhr's theology reflected this distinction between contextualism and dogmatism. His work, therefore, not only helps to expose the fallacies in the Enlightenment interpretation of reason, but also offers a model for a public inquiry that acknowledges the historicity of human life and thought. The implications of this model of public inquiry for theological reflection are most readily seen, in my view, in *Radical Monotheism*. This is true despite some of his own comments, which obscured the form of argumentation that is operative in the text.

Niebuhr repeatedly stressed, for instance, that theological reflection is inseparable from faith, that it does not presume to move inferentially from reason to faith. "[W]hen we carry on theological work," he claimed, "we must do so as men who participate in faith."[7] Although such passages can easily be misinterpreted, Niebuhr's point was not that the theologian uncritically appropriates a given faith, dogmatically embracing it as the presupposition for all future inquiry. On the contrary, he was calling attention to the contextual nature of theological reflection.

The reasoning of the theologian is informed by faith in two senses. First, like all reflection, theology does not proceed from some neutral standpoint but presupposes an underlying faith commitment or value center. Faith, understood as "the attitude and action of confidence in, and fidelity to, certain realities as the sources of value and the objects of loyalty," is operative in all that we think and do.[8] Faith, in this sense, is not peculiar to theological reflection. No human life or thought can escape from an implicit commitment to some center of value from which action and inquiry proceed.

Second, theological reflection is dependent upon the faith of specific traditions. The theologian does not think in a vacuum, but within the history of a particular community of faith. This does not prevent a critical assessment of communal history. As Niebuhr put it, reason "organizes, compares, reflects, criticizes, and develops hypotheses in the midst of believing."[9] Theology, consequently, "doubts some beliefs about God and about man and seeks surer beliefs."[10]

Niebuhr's analysis of the various forms of human faith in *Radical Monotheism* exhibits dependence upon these two senses of faith. The analysis does not even pretend to proceed from a neutral, objective standpoint, but emphasizes from the start the inescapable

---

[7] H. Richard Niebuhr, *Radical Monotheism and Western Culture* (New York: Harper and Row, 1970), 13.

[8] Ibid., 16.

[9] Ibid., 13.

[10] Ibid., 14.

influence of our value commitments. Nor does it presume to examine the meaning and implications of monotheistic faith apart from the historic traditions that have been, at least for the author, the vehicle of this orientation. Nevertheless, despite Niebuhr's acknowledgment that his inquiry was rooted in a tradition of interpretation, his defense of radical monotheistic faith was not limited to demonstrating its centrality within the history of the Christian community. Nor did he appeal to scriptural, ecclesiastical, or narrowly experiential criteria to justify it. On the contrary, he developed a powerful argument for the greater adequacy of radical monotheism in the formation of selves and communities by assessing the pragmatic repercussions of alternate faiths in the spheres of politics, science, and religion.

The Meaning of Revelation constitutes a theoretical articulation and defense of the form of theological reflection embodied in *Radical Monotheism*. The predominant emphasis in this earlier text was upon the historical and social location of human inquiry, an emphasis which, at least in my case, long fostered a confessional reading of Niebuhr's theological method. Indeed, Niebuhr's appropriation of "confessional" to designate his approach has helped to obscure his recognition of the critical and creative dimensions in theological reflection. Although insisting that all reflection necessarily operates in a particular time and place, and through a particular language, he repeatedly warned against the temptations of "national, racial and ecclesiastical relativism" which "proclaims that only the thought and experience of a particular historical group is true and dependable."[11] A confessional approach, as Niebuhr understood it, did not preclude "the work of self-criticism and self-knowledge."[12]

This becomes especially clear in Niebuhr's treatment of internal and external history, both of which incorporated a critical component. Internal history, the cumulative narrative through which the self and the community interpret their past and experience their present, is neither static nor incorrigible. As a communal possession it demands a process of social verification. Lest his confessional theology be confused with arbitrary subjectivism, Niebuhr warned that "subjectivity here is not equivalent to isolation, non-

---

[11] H. Richard Niebuhr, *The Meaning of Revelation* (New York: Macmillan, 1941), 12.
[12] Ibid., 13.

verifiability and ineffability; our history can be communicated and persons can refresh as well as criticize each other's memories of what has happened to them in the common life."[13]

Although communal corroboration and criticism are crucial for sustaining the life and well-being of the community, they are not sufficent. Given the commitment to monotheism which makes all perspectives relative, they must be supplemented by an engagement with external history, with perspectives that do not share the insider's point of view. As Niebuhr wrote, "every external history of ourselves, communicated to us, becomes an event in inner history."[14] Although sometimes the proper response may be defense, it may also be the occasion for "self-criticism and reformation."[15]

The "confessionalism" Niebuhr advocated was not a cloak for fideism but a reactive strategy aimed at dismantling the Enlightenment pretensions to universality, objectivity, and neutrality. He was most concerned to undermine an unbridled confidence in a reason that transcended its social and historical location. At the same time, however, he sought to guard against the temptations peculiar to historicist reason: the retreat to dogmatic self-assurance or skeptical despair about the limitations of reason. Both reactions abandon the task of critical reflection, the former by assuming one is in possession of the truth, the latter by assuming that a reason without universal pretensions has lost its critical edge.[16]

A Niebuhrian theologian belongs to the species Michael Walzer has recently called the "connected critic." Rather than requiring detachment from a form of life, the connected critic is one who enters, either actually or imaginatively, "into local practices and arrangements,"[17] who is familiar with a way of life, with the historical narratives of a people, with the ideals and fears that motivate

[13] Ibid., 53.

[14] Ibid., 62.

[15] Ibid., 62.

[16] Niebuhr's position anticipates a perspective that has become increasingly prevalent within philosophy. See, e.g., Richard J. Bernstein, *Beyond Objectivism and Relativism* (Philadelphia: University of Pennsylvania Press, 1983); Alasdair MacIntyre, *Whose Justice? Which Rationality?* (Notre Dame, Indiana: University of Notre Dame Press, 1988); Jeffrey Stout, *The Flight From Authority* (Notre Dame, Indiana: University of Notre Dame Press, 1981).

[17] Michael Walzer, *Interpretation and Social Criticism* (Cambridge, Massachusetts: Harvard University Press, 1987), 39.

them. Such familiarity with a community and its history is what makes relevant and persuasive criticism possible. As Niebuhr wrote, "freedom from the past or newness of understanding and movement toward more fitting response does not come through the rejection of the past but through its reinterpretation."[18] Connection with a tradition, therefore, is not simply a conservative ploy. It is, potentially, the basis for radical change. In Niebuhr's words, "No great change in political or economic life has ever taken place without a recollection of the past; no new freedom has ever been won without appeal to an old freedom, nor any right established save as an ancient right denied by intervening tyranny."[19]

Further indication that Niebuhr was seeking to demarcate a form of inquiry grounded in traditions of interpretation without capitulating to their authority is reflected in his dilemma over appropriate labels for his work. In the prologue to *The Responsible Self*, for instance, he struggled to find a designation for his contextual but nondogmatic inquiry into the moral life. He explained: "My approach to the subject is neither theological nor philosophical in the sense in which these terms are employed for the most part by professional workers in both groups. Since neither recognizes the logical or academic legitimacy of a 'Christian moral philosophy,' neither will be led to expect anything here of which he might want to take account."[20] His form of reflection did not fit the mold, as he then perceived it, of philosophy or theology. As he explained several pages later, philosophers tend to proceed oblivious to their social and historical location, and theologians tend toward a dogmatic biblicism insofar as they continue to "deal with the Scriptures as a nonhistorical book and undertake to explain it as though they were nonhistorical men."[21]

Niebuhr's work helps us to see that particularity need not preclude publicness. A false pretension to universality and objectivity has obscured the historical determinants in all forms of inquiry, thereby enthroning an impossible model for public inquiry. Overthrowing this model makes way for an alternate interpretation

---

[18] H. Richard Niebuhr, *The Responsible Self* (New York: Harper and Row, 1963), 104.

[19] Niebuhr, *Meaning of Revelation*, 4.

[20] Niebuhr, *Responsible Self*, 42.

[21] Ibid., 46.

of public reflection, one that acknowledges the dependence of inquiry upon local contexts and narratives. Niebuhr's professed "confessionalism" is, in my view, a misleading characterization of the approach he actually adopted. It conjures up too readily an uncritical embrace of a particular narrative, playing down the role criticism and reformation have in continuing the narrative. Niebuhr can more accurately be viewed as defending what I would call an extensional theology.

In this understanding of theology, the theologian operates as a social critic, seeking to sustain, interpret, critique, and reform a particular religious worldview and its concomitant way of life. If the theologian engages in open inquiry rather than citation, this form of theology can be considered, as easily as, say, philosophy, ethics, or literary criticism, a genre of public reflection.

IV

Public theology, however, incorporates more than a public form of inquiry. It also includes a substantive agenda that differentiates it from other theologies. Simply put, the task of a public theology is to contribute to the upbuilding and the critical transformation of our public life. In one sense this means overcoming the privatization of religion and theological reflection, refusing to confine them to issues of personal and interpersonal spirituality. Such a negative characterization, however, is insufficient. It fails to identify the nature of the public life that stands overagainst the private. I would offer a more careful characterization which does not simply affirm the sense of public that we most readily would contrast to the private. Just as the parochial/public polarity needed to be deconstructed to articulate a more adequate interpretation of public, now it is necessary to reinterpret the public counterpart to the private sphere.

Our interpretation of the public, as I noted earlier, has been shaped in response to the Enlightenment and its emancipatory and irenic aims. The success of this project was in large part dependent upon the overthrow of traditional political, social and ecclesiastical authorities. To this end the freedom and autonomy of the individual were stressed, giving birth to a contractual form of society in lieu of a communal one. This transition meant that instead of being regarded as a common body possessing a shared vision of the good, the public was increasingly construed as a collection of individuals pursuing their self-interest. Any communal sense of a public life eroded under this vision of the autonomous, self-interested individual.

This modern trajectory has led some theorists to speak of the eclipse of the public sphere in the contemporary world. John Dewey, for instance, contended that the modernizing forces that destroyed the older local forms of communal life simultaneously eroded a public realm. These forces helped produce a "great society," a vast and complex form of life with "lasting, extensive and serious consequences of associated activity."[22] They did not generate, however, an organized, conversant public body to explore and debate the far reaching effects of this vast associational life. Hannah Arendt argued similarly that the public realm has been absorbed by a society of mass conformism. We have lost the sense of a public whose commonality does not eradicate individual differences.[23] More recently, in *Habits of the Heart* Robert Bellah and his co-authors called our attention to the erosion in American life of the communal traditions which have historically tempered the individualism of the classical liberalism reflected in our political institutions and economic arrangements.

These voices help to identify the nature of the public that needs to be created. In particular they help to show that it is not simply the political as such that can alleviate the spiral of individualism and collectivism that characterizes modernity. Although a political agenda also moves beyond the private sphere, it typically rests upon the prevailing sense of the public as a collectivity of autonomous, self-interested individuals. Hence, more often than not, it reflects the jockeying for power of another special interest group. A public theology, therefore, is not simply a theology with a political agenda, despite the fact that it shares the aim of overcoming the privatization of religion. A public theology seeks to move beyond a "minimal vision of what is possible among people," recognizing that "if we envision the public as nothing more than a battleground between divergent self-interests, we create a dismal self-fulfilling prophecy."[24] A public theology seeks to cultivate a sense of com-

---

[22] John Dewey, *The Public and Its Problems* (Chicago: Swallow Press, 1927), 67.

[23] Arendt, *The Human Condition*, 56–58.

[24] Parker J. Palmer, *The Company of Strangers* (New York: Crossroad, 1981), 36.

mon life as the indispensable basis for political activity.

Niebuhr, perhaps more than any theologian with whom I am familiar, directed attention to this common life within which we all, whether knowingly or not, exist. Furthermore, he provided an extensive theological rationale for it, demonstrating why trust and loyalty in one God necessarily entails a recognition of and commitment to the interconnected network of being. For these reasons his work is a particularly useful guide for our continuing efforts to break out of the privatization of religion. Indeed, it is especially relevant today as a corrective to those political theologies whose efforts to combat the privatization of religion fall short of a reconstruction of the underlying private and public topography that informs our intellectual and social life.

For Niebuhr, radical monotheism not only entailed a recognition of the interconnectedness of all being, but also elicited a reverence for its worth. The unity and value of being are attributed to the power by which being is -- the creative divine source. Faithful loyalty to the divine source, the One beyond the many, manifests itself in loyalty to the realm of being. As Niebuhr wrote, "the principle of being has a cause, namely, the realm of being, so that loyalty to the principle of being must include loyalty to its cause."[25] More specifically, loyalty to the principle of being serves not only to relativize the realm of being, but also to valorize it. Loyalty to the One beyond the many means that "no special places, times, persons, or communities are more representative of the One than any others are."[26] Although radical monotheism produces an extreme iconoclasm, it simultaneously leads to the "sanctification of all things" by virtue of their dependence upon the creative source of being for existence itself.

A radically monotheistic faith engenders a recognition of a community of being that remains, regardless of the indifference, disagreement, and betrayals of its members. This community is rooted in the possession of a common source or center, the power of being by which all beings exist. Commitment to the community of being and to God as its source precludes turning conflicts and schisms into absolute divisions. It encourages self-scrutiny and repentance in the face of conflicts, and prohibits regarding any

---

[25] Niebuhr, *Radical Monotheism*, 33.
[26] Ibid., 52.

person, group, or sphere as ultimately irredeemable.[27] For Niebuhr, our common life, established by the divine creative source, preceded the political, social, and moral divisions that separate us. Considering it coextensive with the realm of being itself, Niebuhr specifically warned against reducing it to a spiritual realm or a Christian sectarianism, noting that "the line between church and world runs through every soul, not between souls."[28]

Niebuhr's theology not only contributes to recent efforts to overcome the privatization of religion. It also provides a more fundamental critique of the private and public geography with which it is intertwined. His work carries out an important task of public theology as I understand it: to build and nurture a sense of common life, a vision of interdependence that precedes the political. To limit public theology to such a task, however, runs the risk of defending a highly reactionary ideology that provides a sacred canopy for all manner of inequities. Too much focus on the common life that we share, or the community of being within which we exist, obscures the blatant treason that marks the life of this community. We need to consider, in other words, how recognition of a common life provides a basis for moral and political judgment. Although Niebuhr's theology is extremely effective in its evocation and defense of the community of being, I find it much more ambiguous in its implications for the critical transformation of this public life.

Niebuhr's theology is ambiguous on this issue because it contains two different strands, not easily harmonized, which have markedly different implications for moral and political critique. The first strand, focusing upon God's sovereignty and providence, functions primarily to relativize the finite order, and provides little impetus or direction for moral and political judgments. When this strand predominated, Niebuhr essentially denied the validity of relative value judgments. In this vein he could write, "All the relative judgments of worth are equalized in the presence of this One who loves all and hates all, but whose love like whose hatred is without emotion, without favoritism."[29] Indeed, Niebuhr suggested

---

[27] This emphasis is particularly strong in the following articles: "The Grace of Doing Nothing," *The Christian Century* 49 (1932) 378–80; "War as Crucifixion," *The Christian Century* 60 (1943) 513–15; and "War as the Judgment of God," *The Christian Century* 59 (1942) 630–33.

[28] Niebuhr, *Faith on Earth* (New Haven: Yale University Press, 1989), 117.

[29] Niebuhr, *Radical Monotheism*, 123.

that the very effort to make judgments is at the root of human sin: "The cross does not so much reveal that God judges by other standards than men do, but that he does not judge; it does not demonstrate that men judge by the wrong standards but that their wrongness lies in trying to judge each other."[30] This relativizing of human values and judgments led him to place repentence and forgiveness at the core of Christian action, and to warn that our task is "not that of building utopias."[31]

There is another trajectory in Niebuhr's theology, however, that has significantly different implications for social critique. In this trajectory, anthropocentrism is again dethroned, finite judgments are relativized, and repentence and forgiveness are also made the cornerstone of the Christian life. But rather than stopping here, Niebuhr moved on to a consideration of what happens on the other side of this iconoclastic moment. He not only recognized the inevitability but also insisted upon the legitimacy of operating out of a variety of relative value systems, all the while recognizing their limited, provisional character. He wrote:

> It is true that if I consider only the value my neighbor has to God and ignore his value for other men, there will be no room for relative justice or for any kind of justice. But in that case I am not acting with piety but with impiety . . . But if I consider him in his value-relations to all his neighbors and also in his value-relation to God, then there is room not only for relative justice but for the formation and reformation of relative judgments by reference to the absolute relation.[32]

Niebuhr's reflections on the appropriate Christian response to the Second World War embodied this dialectical approach. Emphasizing the judgment of God upon all parties in the war, Niebuhr again insisted upon the need for self-scrutiny, repentence, and forgiveness. Yet this initial response does not preclude the responsibility to perform one's duty in the specific situation, to engage in "resistance to those who are abusing our neighbors."[33] Protecting others from injustice thus becomes an important direc-

---

[30] Niebuhr, "War as Crucifixion," 515.

[31] Niebuhr, "The Only Way Into the Kingdom of God," *The Christian Century* 49 (1932) 447.

[32] Niebuhr, *Christ and Culture* (New York: Harper and Row, 1951), 240.

[33] Niebuhr, "War as the Judgment of God," 632.

tive in the continual struggle to locate reflection and action within a universal context. This would suggest that moral activity is not limited to repentence and forgiveness, but is directed toward the creation of a universal community. This more positive specification of appropriate response to the absolute appears to underlie Niebuhr's observation that "faith in God cannot become incarnate except in a universal community in which all walls of partition have been broken down."[34]

The first strand in Niebuhr's theology, emphasizing the absoluteness of God rather than the dialectic between the universal and the finite, does not provide an adequate basis for a public theology. For while it contributes to the restoration of a common life, it does not provide the grounds for its critique and transformation. This limitation is rooted, in my judgment, in Niebuhr's understanding of the divine nature and activity. His stress upon divine sovereignty and power undercuts human agency, suggesting that the latter can only impede, not facilitate, the divine agenda. He appears to posit a divine creative process that is hampered, not furthered, by human efforts. As a consequence, the appropriate human response to divine activity is to acquire a deterministic understanding of divine providence:

> The self which is one in itself responds to all actions upon it as expressive of One intention or One context. For it there is no evil in the city but the Lord has done it; no crucifixion but the One has crucified. How and why these events fit in, it does not yet know. So far as it acknowledges in positive or negative faith, in trust or distrust, the One in the many, it accepts the presence only of One action in all actions upon it.[35]

Such an understanding of the divine agency nurtures an acquiescent spirit, a sense that somehow things are, from the perspective of the creative power, as they should be. It does not, in my judgment, provide the necessary ground or motivation for political and social critique.

The second strand in Niebuhr's theology, which emphasizes the dialectic between the absolute and the finite, is conducive to the development of a public theology that can both create and critique

---

34 Niebuhr, *Radical Monotheism*, 62.
35 Niebuhr, *Responsible Self*, 125–26.

a common life. Although this strand is not reconcilable with many of Niebuhr's observations about divine power and agency, it is, in other respects, substantially grounded in his interpretation of God. Indeed, as I struggle to articulate an understanding of God in the process of developing a public theology, I find many of his reflections about the divine nature most persuasive, particularly his locating the referent for God in the power that sustains and orders life.

I would avoid intimations, however, that this power exists over against the many, stressing instead its embodiment in being. This emphasis on immanence remains responsive to the wonder that there is something rather than nothing, and to the inescapable feeling that there is some evolutionary impulse at work in the cosmos. Emphasizing its presence in all of creation helps to thwart the anthropocentrism that Niebuhr rightly noted infects our lives, with increasingly dangerous results. But stressing the immanent power of Being in sustaining and ordering life makes it possible to see how human agency contributes to this activity, albeit in a very circumscribed way. Although human beings obviously operate with the limitations and self-deceptions of finite creatures, they can participate in the struggles to establish an interconnected network of being in which each life form is graced with life and the possibility of contributing to the universal community of being.

This vision of the universal community is more than an ideal and less than a reality. The interdependence into which we are thrust by virtue of life itself suggests that our common life is more than a wishful projection. But the even more obvious presence of discord, oppression, and betrayal painfully indicates the eschatalogical dimension of this vision. By identifying the divine spirit in relationship to the sustaining power of being and to the ordering processes in which beings participate, I am seeking to distinguish between the common life as our ground, and the universal community as our goal.

The task of a public theology, then, is twofold: first, it seeks to elicit an acknowledgment of a common public life that underlies and precedes political, social, and moral divisions. It undertakes this task out of the conviction that the absence of a sense of such a common life produces divisive, un-self-critical, and dogmatic political and moral factions. A public theology, however, also seeks to facilitate political, social, and moral critiques of the common life in an effort to transform that life in the direction of the universal community. Niebuhr's work is particularly effective in carrying out the first step. The implications of his thought for the second step are less clear.

V

Thus far I have been developing a model for a public theology in terms of its methodological characteristics and its substantive agenda. A theology can fail to be truly public, however, in another important way. Whether or not it avoids sliding into parochialism or privatism, a theology can adopt such a professionalized style that, for all intents and purposes, it loses all claim to being a form of public discourse. If theology is to have any success at overcoming its cultural marginalization, it must pay more attention to questions of style and audience. It is pointless for theologians to denounce their shrinking audience when much that they write is unintelligible outside, if not inside, their own professional guild.

The style of most theological writing reflects the academic audience at which it is aimed. Extensive references to the literature and endless qualifying footnotes have become the hallmark of this form of writing. Perhaps even more problematic is the tendency to adopt the jargon of particular schools of philosophy or theology, thereby limiting even further the accessibility of one's work.

The problems of excessive professionalization are not peculiar to the field of theology, of course. But succumbing to the institutional and intellectual pressures that have fostered specialized and technical studies is, for theology, as for philosophy, self-defeating. Lacking the practical applications of sophisticated and technical studies in the natural and social sciences, a highly professionalized theology risks becoming an insulated and ineffective form of discourse perpetuated by an elite.

A public theology, of course, does not mean a theology that is intelligible to every single person, the way a public park is open to all. As a form of critical reflection, it presupposes a literate, informed audience. This element of elitism is an inevitable component of intellectual disciplines. But much theology, it seems to me, has moved far beyond this level, abandoning all presumption of communicating with a general educated public. Often, when a text is addressed to a general readership, it is regarded as a "popular" work whose contents are derivative rather than original.

Niebuhr's work is instructive on this issue for it embodies a style of theological reflection that does not limit it to a single professional guild. He made minimal reference to other texts, and refrained from appropriating specialized vocabulary intelligible only to the initiates of a particular school or thinker. Perhaps most importantly, his work is unmistakable testimony to the fact that a theology accessible to a general readership does not automatically render it a piece of popularizing.

No doubt the location of much contemporary theological writing within the university accounts for its increasing professionalization. The need, both institutionally and psychologically, to produce work that appears scholarly to colleagues in other academic disciplines exacerbates the problem. Continuing to deal with matters of the religious life within the modern secular university may add impetus to the embrace of an impeccable scholarly facade. While these forces have facilitated the historical and comparative study of religion, they have tended to paralyze theology by stifling its creative urges.

VI

The forces that have contributed to the cultural marginalization of religion and theology are varied, complex, and not easily reversed. They have helped to erect a vision of the public that continues to dominate our sensibilities, despite the erosion of its emancipatory power. A number of voices, however, have begun to challenge the privatization of religion, demanding a greater role for religious beliefs and values in shaping public life. These voices, reflecting both liberationist and fundamentalist perspectives, have played an extremely important role in exposing the interests that have been served by confining religion to a private or spiritual realm.

Many of these voices have been more successful in their criticisms of the privatization of religion than in their proposals for overcoming it. In part this is due to a failure to engage in public forms of argumentation in the defense of such proposals. I suspect, however, that a further problem lies in a tendency to turn liberalism on its head in order to thwart its modern trajectory. Rejecting the radical individualism of liberalism, with its accompanying privatization of values and ends, a presumption of a common vision of the good, with divine sanction, is too easily embraced as an alternative. Not surprisingly, those who do not share the perspective recoil in horror at the prospect of religion emerging from its private haven.

Niebuhr's work helps significantly to articulate the positive role that religion and theology can play in the public realm. His contribution to this debate is rooted, in my judgment, in his implicit reconfiguration of the public/private geography that currently prevails. This is evident, first, in the very way in which he made his case. He engaged in a form of reflection that remained self-critical and open even as it acknowledged the inescapable influence of traditions of interpretation. His is a model of public inquiry that reflects a historicist interpretation of reason.

Niebuhr's implicit rejection of the prevailing public and private landscape is also evident in the content of the religious vision that he advanced. Far from construing the public as a collection of atomistic individuals, Niebuhr emphasized the interdependent network of being that is centered in and by the divine creative source. His radically monotheistic perspective, in other words, generates a vision of a common public life that is far removed from the individualistic bias of the prevailing outlook. But this understanding of the public impact of religion does not presume to identify any particular political or moral strategy as divinely sanctioned. On the contrary, Niebuhr was primarily concerned with combating the perennial temptation to sacralize a political or moral stance by identifying it too closely with the divine perspective. Niebuhr's contribution to the controversy over the public impact of religion, in other words, lies in his efforts to restore a sense of public life that precedes political divisions, thereby countering the factionalism and dogmatism of those divisions.

If Niebuhr has refocused our attention on the perennial dangers of idolatry, however, liberation theologians have been equally persuasive in exposing the perennial tendency of religion to sanction the status quo. We have to consider whether Niebuhr's success in highlighting a common public life comes at the expense of political and moral critique. In one sense his preoccupation with the dangers of idolatry and his emphasis on the interconnected network of being leave such an impression. The more serious question, for his theology and for the quest for a public theology, however, is whether this result is inevitable. I have tried to argue that it is not, but this depends greatly upon the interpretation of God, particularly the divine power and agency, that one embraces. To avoid the twin perils of idolatry and sanctioning the status quo, a public theology should strive to elicit a recognition of a common life within which all co-exist without forgetting that that life remains a foretaste and shadow of its ultimate form. To make this case publicly and persuasively constitutes the challenge and the task of a public theology.

8

Response to Linell Cady

Robin W. Lovin

Professor Cady's paper is both an important discussion of the task of public theology and an accurate assessment of the strengths and weaknesses of H. Richard Niebuhr's contributions to it. I find myself very much in agreement with her assessment that Niebuhr's public theology offers a strong statement of the absoluteness of God's judgment on all human aims and institutions, and a rather weaker discernment of critical standards for evaluating the options among which we actually have to choose. What I want to do, as a prelude to more general discussion, is to focus on Professor Cady's broader question of the tasks of public theology, in the hope that a restatement of some of the issues she has raised might also give us a slightly different angle of vision on Niebuhr's contribution.

Professor Cady formulates the problem of public theology in terms of tasks and problems that are rather specific to the theological enterprise, and here I think that she has correctly identified our recurrent professional anxieties. Theologians seek a public theology as a way to escape the narrow, dogmatic exposition which the Enlightenment assigned to them. If, as Kant said, the Enlightenment began with an awakening from dogmatic slumbers, all too many Enlightenment thinkers have sent the theologians off to permanent nap time, and the theologians have come to resent it. One expects, of course, that there will be pointed disagreements with those who do not share religious convictions, but theologians have understandably grown touchy about the secularists' off-handed assumption that theological claims cannot even make sense to those who do not share theological premises.

For some, as Professor Cady points out, this touchiness takes the form of an effort to demonstrate that theology, too, can be a meta-discourse, certifiably as specialized in its own professional vocabulary and as remote from ordinary language as the specialized disciplines of philosophy, linguistics, social theory, and political science. Others, however, have taken the more helpful and productive route of public theology, speaking about the meaning of a religious tradition in terms that make sense to, and elicit response from, people who do not share theological convictions.

Professor Cady thus catches some of the special problems of theology as a form of public discourse, but that way of posing the issue may also make it seem that the problems of theology are unique. Let me suggest an alternative starting point. Perhaps the most difficult questions today concern not the public character of theology, but the very existence of that public intellectual forum that theology is supposed to be seeking to enter. It is an inheritance of old Enlightenment controversies that universities still contain persons who insist that theology is in some particular way unsuited to the tasks of a community of rational discourse, but these persons are historical survivals, rather like the sheriff of Middlesex County at a Harvard commencement. They remind us of how things were. They do not raise the important contemporary questions.

Those contemporary questions cut across many fields. A whole range of interpretive disciplines, not just theology, are struggling to formulate alternatives to the Enlightenment definitions of their tasks, and even the hard sciences are caught up in this basic rethinking. This reformulation goes on because the Enlightenment definitions of what our studies are about seem not to work. They do not tell us how the process of scientific discovery, or the interpretation of texts and traditions, or the formation of political communities really happens.

Rethinking those issues raises important questions within each of the academic disciplines, but it also raises for all of them a question of public discourse. That question is far more comprehensive than the one the Enlightenment posed to theology. The Enlightenment assumed that there is a realm of public discourse, defined by criteria of rational and empirical investigation. The question was whether theology could be admitted to it. But if in fact we neither reason as the Enlightenment told us we do, nor restrict our knowledge claims to empirical truths as the Enlightenment told us we must, then what has become of the *public* discourse the Enlightenment defined? Does it still exist? Did it ever exist?

Those questions vex all disciplines, not just theology, and I do not think we have any really good, widely shared answers to them at present. What we have done in lieu of formulating those answers is sometimes to disparage the notion of public discourse altogether, rejecting it in Christian theological circles as a relic of our Constantinian past. Or we have adopted an exceedingly elastic definition of the "public," which will expand or contract to cover just as large a community of discourse as we are able to get. "Public" now contrasts to "private"—individualized or solipsistic—not to "confessional" or "dogmatic." Shared meanings become "public" just as soon as enough people share them. So, for example, when Richard Neuhaus sets out to clothe the "naked public square," he gathers the garments from the closets of the "Judeo-Christian consensus." That consensus seems to acquire this public role largely because so many people believe it is true. In the absence of any more clearly stated understanding of what makes an argument public, "public" comes to apply to anything that is not clearly private, even though it retains its older, normative import of "commanding assent from people generally."

Professor Cady's paper reveals, at least at one point, this tension that vexes all of us who want to continue to talk about public theology at a time when the concept of the public is itself elusive. As Professor Cady summarizes, the task of public theology is "to sustain, interpret, critique, and reform a particular religious world view and its concomitant way of life." Now that is obviously more than an individual or a strictly private undertaking, particularly where the definition of a "faith" or a "religious world view" is as encompassing as it was for Niebuhr. But note that we have here a public that seems to consist of the large number of persons who happen to share a particular religious worldview. I don't think it is the same public that Professor Cady intends later when she says public theology has a "substantive agenda" that involves the "upbuilding and critical transformation of our public life."

You see the tension—on the one hand, a context of reflection centered on a particular worldview; on the other, a context of action involving the transformation of a public that cuts across a number of different "faiths" or "religious worldviews." Professor Cady is surely right to say that theologians must not let Enlightenment-oriented minds tell them that their thinking cannot be public because it is contextual. Theologians are no worse off than anyone else on that score. But the question lies precisely there. How bad off are we? Many thinkers who would be prepared to accept theology as contextual reflection would deny it the transformative role in public life that Professor Cady delineates. They do this not because they think there is some peculiar defect in theology, but because they doubt that there is any truly public life there to be transformed.

In addition to the interpretation of particular religious worldviews and the transformation of public life, then, we may identify a third task which any public theology must undertake. It must help us to understand a public world in which discourse contributes to the solution of public problems. This task is, perhaps, logically prior to the substantive tasks of political theology, but we need not assume that the prior question has to be completely answered before we proceed to the substantive one. In practical reasoning, it often turns out not only that a tentative answer to the prior question allows you to proceed with the substantive question, but also that forging ahead in that way is the best way to test the prior answer. Initially, all we need is some answer to the question of what makes a public theology public, an answer that goes beyond the claims of custom or the power of majorities, moral or otherwise.

For this task, too, there are resources in the work of Niebuhr, and I hope it will contribute to our general discussion if I mention just two of them. First, Niebuhr speaks about a world of common human experience without abolishing the diversity of interpretations or reducing the commonality to an empirically verifiable materialism. Put in his own terms, Niebuhr's account of knowledge is a "theocentric relativism." Put in the jargon of contemporary philosophy, it is an epistemology which strives to be realistic without being foundationalist. We might even call

Niebuhr's account of the public world a "Christian realism," if that term were not so thoroughly identified with certain political tenets of Reinhold Niebuhr's thought.

It is worth remembering, however, that before Christian realism was a political doctrine, it was an idea that D.C. Macintosh, Walter Marshall Horton, and others—including the young H. Richard Niebuhr—called "theological realism" or "realistic theology." That generation insisted that their realism was suspicious of metaphysical or ontological claims. They rejected absolutist moral principles derived from a static "nature." They recognized the contribution of culture and individual imagination to every construction of reality, and so they rejected all accounts of knowledge that makes persons out to be passive observers of what Hilary Putnam calls a "ready-made world."

But they never doubted that there was a world there, constraining our interpretations of it and transcending the contextuality of our thinking. There is no absolute knowledge of the world (or of the human good, or of anything else that we might argue about in public terms). But there is at any given time a finite set of competing accounts of it, and these accounts are not merely alternative contexts. They make claims about reality that can be assessed. The principal method of assessment is *pragmatic*: which of the available, real options most effectively guides action over a long period of time? Part of what makes a theology public, then, is this pragmatic conception of a world that theology is about, this notion that that world and what other people say about it sets a critical limit on our own contextual reflections.

Second, Niebuhr contributes to our understanding of public theology an acute sociological sensitivity to the plurality of each person's contextualizations. Professor Cady's paper quotes the fine line from *Faith on Earth* in which Niebuhr reminds us that "the line between church and world runs through every soul, not between souls." The relativity in Niebuhr's theocentric relativism derives not from the variety of religious and cultural contexts in which different people live, but from the awareness that each person lives in several of those contexts at once. We are not fully integrated centers of reflection astonished by the discovery that there are others who see the world differently from ourselves. We understand the pluralism of our social context in part because it reflects the variety of ways in which we understand our own experience.

Faith posits a center of value that it cannot completely grasp; that is what keeps a theocentric relativism from flying apart in a shower of fragmentary perceptions. Faith in that ultimate unity gives me a critical perspective on my own social location, but that social location also gives me a critical perspective on the tentative and partial formulations of my theology. Theocentric relativism is refined, not only in the dialogue between different faith perspectives, but also in the dialogue that goes on within each faithful person.

Public theology, then, must live in the tension between its tasks of interpreting particular religious worldviews and transforming public life, but it must also conduct a dialogue between faith and world in a way that demonstrates the possibility of public theology. It is characteristic of our post-Enlightenment world that these critical questions can no longer be answered by some third discipline that inserts itself into our reasoning before theology and public discourse, to prove that both are possible. Today, one demonstrates the possibility of any kind of discourse by engaging in it, and for that task the practitioners of public theology still have much to learn from the generation of H. Richard Niebuhr.

A Selected Bibliography

More complete listings of H. Richard Niebuhr's work can be found in:

Paul Ramsey, ed. *Faith and Ethics: The Theology of H. Richard Niebuhr.* New York: Harper & Row [1957], 1965, 291–301. This bibliography, compiled in 1957 by Raymond P. Morris and revised in 1964 by Mr. Morris and Jane E. McFarland, includes an extensive section on book reviews by H. Richard Niebuhr, as well as reviews and criticism of the writings of H. Richard Niebuhr;

Libertus A. Hoedemaker. *The Theology of H. Richard Niebuhr.* Philadelphia: Pilgrim Press [1970], 1979, 196–204. This bibliography was also compiled by Jane E. McFarland and includes a list of selected unpublished materials; and

James W. Fowler. *To See the Kingdom: The Theological Vision of H. Richard Niebuhr.* Nashville: Abingdon Press [1974], 1985, 277–283. A list of selected unpublished materials by H. Richard Niebuhr may also be found here.

A bibliography of the writings of the young H. Richard Niebuhr, held in the archives of Eden Theological Seminary in St. Louis, Missouri, appears in William G. Chrystal, "The Young H. Richard Niebuhr," *Theology Today* 38 (1981) 231–35.

Books

Ernst Troeltsch's Philosophy of Religion. Yale University doctoral dissertation, 1924. Ann Arbor, MI: University Microfilms, Inc., 1986.

The Social Sources of Denominationalism. New York: Henry Holt & Co., 1929. Reprint eds. Hamden, CT: The Shoe String Press, 1954; New York:

Meridian Books, 1957; New York: New American Library, 1975; Gloucester, MA: Peter Smith, 1987.

The Religious Situation, by Paul Tillich. Translated by H. Richard Niebuhr. New York: Henry Holt & Co., 1932. Translator's preface, vii–xxii.

The Church Against the World. With Wilhelm Pauck and Francis P. Miller. Chicago and New York: Willet, Clark & Co., 1935.

The Kingdom of God in America. Chicago and New York: Willett, Clark & Co., 1937. Reprint eds. Hamden, CT: The Shoe String Press, 1956; New York: Harper Torchbooks, 1959; Middletown, CT: Wesleyan University Press, 1988.

The Meaning of Revelation. 1941. Reprint eds. New York: The Macmillan Co., 1946, 1952, 1960, 1978.

Christ and Culture. New York: Harper & Brothers, 1951. Reprint ed. New York: Harper Torchbooks, 1956.

The Purpose of the Church and its Ministry: Reflections on the Aims of Theological Education. With Daniel Day Williams and James M. Gustafson. New York: Harper & Brothers, 1956.

The Ministry in Historical Perspectives. Edited with Daniel Day Williams. New York: Harper & Brothers, 1956.

The Advancement of Theological Education. With Daniel Day Williams and James M. Gustafson. New York: Harper & Brothers, 1957.

Radical Monotheism and Western Civilization. Lincoln: University of Nebraska, 1960.

Radical Monotheism and Western Culture, with Supplementary Essays. New York: Harper & Brothers, 1960. Reprint ed. New York: Harper Torchbooks, 1970.

The Responsible Self: An Essay in Christian Moral Philosophy. 1963. Reprint ed. New York: Harper & Row, 1978. Preface by Richard R. Niebuhr and introduction by James M. Gustafson.

Faith on Earth: An Inquiry into the Structure of Human Faith. Edited by Richard R. Niebuhr. New Haven: Yale University Press, 1989.

Articles in Books and Periodicals

"From the Religion of Humanity to the Religion of God." In *Theological Magazine of the Evangelical Synod of North America,* 57 (1929) 401–09.

Moral Relativism and the Christian Ethic. New York: International Missionary Council, 1929.

"The Irreligion of Communist and Capitalist." In *The Christian Century* 47 (1930) 1306–7.

"Religious Ethics." In *World Tomorrow* 13 (1930) 443–46.

"The Social Gospel and the Liberal Theology." In *The Keryx* 22 (1931) 12–13, 18.

"Religious Realism in the Twentieth Century." In *Religious Realism*, edited by D. C. Macintosh, 413–28. New York: The Macmillan Company, 1931.

"The Grace of Doing Nothing." In *The Christian Century* 49 (1932) 378–80.

"A Communication: The Only Way into the Kingdom of God." In *The Christian Century* 49 (1932) 447.

"What Then Must We Do?" In *The Christian Century Pulpit* 7 (1934) 133–45.

"Man the Sinner." In *The Journal of Religion* 15 (1935) 272–280.

"Toward the Emancipatiton of the Church." In *Christendom* 1 (1935) 133–45.

"The Attack Upon the Social Gospel." In *Religion in Life* 5 (1936) 176–81.

"Value Theory and Theology." In *The Nature of Religious Experience: Essays in Honor of Douglas Clyde Macintosh*, 93–116. New York: Harper & Brothers, 1937.

"Life is Worth Living." In *The Intercollegian and Far Horizons* 57 (1939) 3–4, 22.

"War as the Judgment of God." In *The Christian Century* 59 (1942) 630–33.

"Is God in the War?" In *The Christian Century* 59 (1942) 953–55.

"War as Crucifixion." In *The Christian Century* 60 (1943) 513–15.

"The Hidden Church and the Churches in Sight." In *Religion in Life* 15 (1945) 106–16. Reprinted in *Religion in Life* 47 (1978) 371–80.

"The Ego-Alter Dialectic and the Conscience." In *The Journal of Philosophy* 42 (1945) 352–59.

"The Doctrine of the Trinity and the Unity of the Church." In *Theology Today* 3 (1946) 371–84. A revised version of this paper appears under the title "Theological Unitarianisms" in *Theology Today* 40 (1983) 150–57.

"A Utilitarian Christianity." In *Christianity and Crisis* 6 (1946) 3–5.

"The Norm of the Church." In *Journal of Religious Thought* 4 (1946–47) 5–15.

"The Responsibility of the Church for Society." In *The Gospel, the Church, and the World*, edited by K. S. Latourette, 111–33. New York and London: Harper & Brothers, 1946.

Introduction to *The Essence of Christianity*, by Ludwig Feuerbach, vii–ix. New York: Harper, 1947.

"The Gift of the Catholic Vision." In *Theology Today* 4 (1948) 507–21.

"Evangelical and Protestant Ethics." In *The Heritage of the Reformation*, edited by Elmer J. F. Arndt, 211–29. New York: Richard R. Smith, 1950.

"The Center of Value." In *Moral Principles of Action: Man's Ethical Imperative*, edited by R. N. Anshen, 162–75. New York: Harper & Brothers, 1952.

"The Idea of Covenant and American Democracy." In *Church History* 23 (1954) 126–35.

"The Triad of Faith." In *Andover Newton Bulletin* 47 (1954) 3–12.

"Isolation and Cooperation in Theological Education." In *Theological Education in America* 3 (1955) 1–6.

Christian Ethics: Sources of the Living Tradition. Edited with introductions by Waldo Beach and H. Richard Niebuhr. New York: Ronald Press Co. [1955], 1973.

"Sören Kierkegaard." In *Christianity and the Existentialists*, edited by Carl Donald Michalson, 23–42. New York: Scribner, 1956.

Foreword to *In His Likeness*, by G. McLeod Bryan, 5–6. Richmond, VA: John Knox Press, 1959.

Introduction to *The Social Teaching of the Christian Churches*, by Ernst Troeltsch, 7–12. New York: Harper Torchbooks, 1960. Reprint ed. Chicago: The University of Chicago Press, 1976.

"The Seminary in the Ecumenical Age." In *Theology Today* 17 (1960) 300–10.

"Reformation: Continuing Imperative." In *The Christian Century* 77 (1960) 248–51. Reprinted in *How My Mind Has Changed*, edited by Harold E. Fey, 69–80. Cleveland: World Publishing Co., 1961.

"On the Nature of Faith." In *Religious Experience and Truth: A Symposium*, edited by Sidney Hook, 93–102. New York: New York University Press, 1961.

"The Protestant Movement and Democracy in the United States." In *Religion in American Life: The Shaping of American Religion*, vol. 1, edited by James Ward Smith and A. Leland Jamison, 29–71. Princeton: Princeton University Press, 1961.

"The Illusion of Power." In *The Pulpit* 33 (1962) 4(100) – 7(103).

"The Story of Our Life." In *Interpreting Religion*, by Donald Walhout, 305–14. Englewood Cliffs, NJ: Prentice-Hall, 1963. Reprint of a chapter from *The Meaning of Revelation*.

"Towards a New Otherworldliness." In *Theology Today* 1 (1964) 78–87.

"Reflections on Faith, Hope and Love." In *The Journal of Religious Ethics* 2 (1974) 151–56.

"The Social Gospel and the Mind of Jesus," edited by Diane Yeager. In *The Journal of Religious Ethics* 16 (1988) 115–127.

Books and Articles on H. Richard Niebuhr

Ahlstrom, Sydney E. "H. Richard Niebuhr's Place in American Thought." In *Christianity and Crisis* 23 (1963) 213–17.

Allen, Joseph L. "A Decisive Influence on Protestant Ethics." In *Christianity and Crisis* 23 (1963) 217–19.

Beker, E. J. "The Sovereignty of God in the Thought of H. Richard Niebuhr." In *Nederlands Theologisch Tijdschrift* 15 (1960) 108–30.

Buri, Fritz. *How Can We Still Speak Responsibly of God?* Philadelphia: Fortress Press, 1968. (Appendix: "The Reality of Faith in H. Richard Niebuhr's *The Meaning of Revelation*," 65–83.)

Byrnes, Thomas A. "H. Richard Niebuhr's Reconstruction of Jonathan Edwards' Moral Theology." In *Annual of the Society of Christian Ethics 1985*, edited by A. Anderson, 33–55.

Cady, Linell E. "Theology and Public Discourse." In *Encounter* 49 (1988) 285–296.

_____. "A Model for a Public Theology." In *Harvard Theological Review* 80 (1987) 192–212.

Cauthen, Kenneth. "An Introduction to the Theology of H. Richard Niebuhr." In *Canadian Journal of Theology* 10 (1964) 4–14.

Chrystal, William G. "Samuel D. Press: Teacher of the Niebuhrs." In *Church History* 53 (1984) 504–21.

Conn, Walter E. "H. Richard Niebuhr on 'Responsibility'." In *Thought* 51 (1976) 82–98.

Crouter, Richard E. "H. Richard Niebuhr and Stoicism." In *The Journal of Religious Ethics* 2 (1974) 129–46.

Diefenthaler, Jon. *H. Richard Niebuhr: A Lifetime of Reflections on the Church and the World.* Macon, GA: Mercer University Press, 1986.

Ede, Alfred J. "Revelation and Relativism in the Theology of H. Richard Niebuhr." In *Horizons* 4 (1977) 27–42.

Eister, Allan W. "H. Richard Niebuhr and the Paradox of Religious Organization: A Radical Critique." In *Beyond the Classics*, edited by C. Y. Glock, 355–408. New York: Harper & Row, 1973.

Fadner, Donald E. *The Responsible God: A Study of the Christian Philosophy of H. Richard Niebuhr*. Missoula, MT: Scholars Press, 1975.

Fowler, James W. *To See the Kingdom: The Theological Vision of H. Richard Niebuhr*. Nashville: Abingdon Press [1974], 1985.

Fox, Richard W. "H. Richard Niebuhr's Divided Kingdom." In *American Quarterly* 42 (1990) 93 – 101.

————. "The Niebuhr Brothers and the Liberal Protestant Heritage." In *Religion and twentieth-century American intellectual life*, edited by Michael J. Lacey, 94 – 115. Woodrow Wilson International Center for Scholars. Cambridge and New York: Cambridge University Press, 1989.

Gardner, E. Clinton. "Responsibility and Moral Direction in the Ethics of H. Richard Niebuhr." In *Encounter* 40 (1979) 143 – 68.

Garrett, William R. "The Sociological Theology of H. Richard Niebuhr." In *Religious Sociology*, edited by W. Swatos, 41 – 55. New York: Greenwood Press, 1987.

Godsey, John D. *The Promise of H. Richard Niebuhr*. Philadelphia: J. B. Lippincott Co., 1970.

Grant, C. David. *God the Center of Value: Value Theory in the Theology of H. Richard Niebuhr*. Fort Worth, TX: Christian University Press, 1984.

Grima, George. "Christ and Conversion: H. Richard Niebuhr's Thought, 1933 – 1937." In *Sylloge Excerptorum* 49 (1979) 1 – 29.

Harrison, Beverly Wildung. "H. Richard Niebuhr: Towards a Christian Moral Philosophy." Ph. D. dissertation. Ann Arbor, MI: University Microfilms, Inc., 1974.

Heim, S. Mark. "Prodigal Sons: D. C. Macintosh and the Brothers Niebuhr." In *The Journal of Religion* 65 (1985) 336 – 58.

Hoedemaker, Libertius A. *The Theology of H. Richard Niebuhr*. Philadelphia: Pilgrim Press [1970], 1979.

Holler, Linda. "Is there a thou 'within' nature? A dialogue with H. Richard Niebuhr." In *The Journal of Religious Ethics* 17 (1989) 81 – 102.

Irish, Jerry A. *The Religious Thought of H. Richard Niebuhr*. Atlanta: John Knox Press, 1983.

Johnson, W. Stanley. "A Wesleyan Reading of H. Richard Niebuhr's Theology." In *Wesley Theological Journal* 23 (1990) 81 – 91.

Keiser, R. Melvin. *Recovering the Personal: Religious Language and the Postcritical Quest of H. Richard Niebuhr*. Atlanta: Scholars Press, 1988.

Kliever, Lonnie D. *H. Richard Niebuhr*. Waco, TX: Word Books, 1977.

Kuhn, Helmut. "Conscience and Society." In *The Journal of Religion* 26 (1946) 203 – 14.

Legerton, Winifred. "H. Richard Niebuhr's Radical Monotheism and Christian Feminism." In *Religious Life* 45 (1976) 427–35.

Macintosh, D. C. "Theology, Valuational or Existential?" In *Review of Religion* 6 (1939) 23–44.

McKinney, William J., Jr. "H. Richard Niebuhr and the Question of Human Society." In *Religion in Life* 43 (1974) 362–375.

McLean, Stuart D. "Basic sources and new possibilities: H. Richard Niebuhr's influence on faith development theory." In *Faith Development and Fowler*, edited by Craig Dykstra and Sharon Parks, 157–79. Birmingham, AL: Religious Education Press, 1986.

Mawhinney, John J. "H. Richard Niebuhr and the Reshaping of American Christianity." In *America in Theological Perspective*, edited by T. M. McFadden, 140–62. New York: Seabury Press, 1976.

Miller, Richard B. "H. Richard Niebuhr's War Articles: A Transvaluation of Value." In *The Journal of Religion* 68 (1988) 242–62.

Nabe, Clyde M. "Confessionalism and Philosophy of Religion." In *The American Journal of Theology and Philosophy* 4 (1983) 64–72.

Ottati, Douglas F. "H. Richard Niebuhr's Theocentric Vision of Ultimate Reality and Meaning." In *Ultimate Reality and Meaning* 11 (1988) 267–78.

————. *Meaning and Method in H. Richard Niebuhr's Theology.* Washington, DC.: University Press of America, 1982.

Phibbs, Raymond C. "An Introductory Summary of the Basic Elements in the Thought of H. Richard Niebuhr." In *Brethren Life* 5 (1960) 38–55.

Ramsey, Paul, ed. *Faith and Ethics: The Theology of H. Richard Niebuhr.* New York: Harper & Row [1957], 1965.

————. *Nine Modern Moralists*, 149–79. Englewood Cliffs, NJ: Prentice-Hall, 1962. Reprint ed. Lanham, MD: University Press of America, 1983. (This book reprints a chapter from *Faith and Ethics*.)

Reid, Malcolm. "H. Richard Niebuhr." In *Reformed Theology in America*, edited by D. Wells, 280–98. Grand Rapids, MI: W. B. Eerdmans Publishing Co., 1985.

Richey, Russell E., ed. *Denominationalism.* Nashville: Abingdon, 1977. (See editor's forward, 9–15, and 229–31, introduction to reprint of a chapter from *The Kingdom of God in America*.)

Sandon, Leo. "H. Richard Niebuhr's Principles of Historiography." In *Foundations* 18 (1975) 61–74.

————. "Jonathan Edwards and H. Richard Niebuhr." In *Religious Studies* 12 (1976) 101–15.

Scriven, Charles. *The Transformation of Culture: Christian Social Ethics after H. Richard Niebuhr*. Scottsdale, PA: Herald Press, 1988.

Sedgwick, Timothy F. "Faith and Discernment: Directions in Theological Ethics in the Thought of H. Richard Niebuhr." In *Andover Newton Quarterly* 18 (1977) 111–21.

—————. "Niebuhr's Ethics of Responsibility: A Unified Interpretation." In *St. Luke Journal* 23 (1980) 265–283.

Sica, Joseph F. *God So Loved the World*. Washington, DC.: University Press of America, 1981.

Soper, David Wesley. "The Permanent Revolution; the Theology of Hope of H. Richard Niebuhr." In *Major Voices in American Theology; Six Contemporary Leaders*, 153–90. Philadelphia: Westminster Press, 1953. Reprint ed. Port Washington, NY: Kennikat Press, 1969.

Welch, D. Donald. "A Niebuhrian Contribution to Normative Ethics." In *Encounter* 44 (1983) 341–51.

Williams, Daniel Day. "A Personal and Theological Memoir." In *Christianity and Crisis* 26 (1963) 209–13.

Yeager, Diane M. "On Making the Tree Good: An Apology for a Dispositional Ethics." In *Journal of Religious Ethics* 10 (1982) 103–120.

Contributors

Linell E. Cady is associate professor and chair of the department of religious studies at Arizona State University. Her articles have appeared in such journals as *American Journal of Theology and Philosophy*, *Harvard Theological Review*, and *Union Seminary Quarterly Review*.

Francis Schüssler Fiorenza is Charles Chauncy Stillman Professor of Roman Catholic Theological Studies at Harvard Divinity School. He is the author of *Foundational Theology: Jesus and the Church* (1984), and, with John Galvin, co-editor of the two-volume *Roman Catholic Perspectives* (1991).

Hans Frei was John A. Hoober Professor of Religious Studies at Yale University. His books include *The Eclipse of Biblical Narrative* (1974), and *The Identity of Jesus Christ* (1975).

James M. Gustafson is Henry R. Luce Professor of Humanities and Comparative Studies at Emory University. His books include *Christ and the Moral Life* (1968), *Protestant and Roman Catholic Ethics* (1978), and the two-volume *Ethics from a Theocentric Perspective* (1981 and 1984).

William R. Hutchison is Charles Warren Professor of the History of Religion in America at Harvard Divinity School. He has written and edited several books, most recently *Between the Times: The Travail of the Protestant Establishment in America, 1900–1960* (1989).

Gordon D. Kaufman is Edward Mallinckrodt Jr. Professor of Divinity at Harvard Divinity School. His books include *An Essay on Theological Method* (1975), *The Theological Imagination: Constructing the Concept of God* (1981), and *Theology for a Nuclear Age* (1985).

Robin W. Lovin is associate professor of religious ethics at the Divinity School of the University of Chicago. He is the author of *Christian Faith and Public Choices* (1984), and has edited and contributed to a number of other volumes on the public role of religion in America.

Harry S. Stout is Professor of American Religious History and John B. Madden Master of Berkeley College at Yale University. He is the author of *The New England Soul: Preaching and Religious Culture in Colonial New England* (1986), and, with Nathan O. Hatch, the editor of *Jonathan Edwards and the American Experience* (1988).

Index of Names and Titles